THE LEADERSHIP COACH

Tony Buon

The Teach Yourself series has been trusted around the world for over 60 years. It has helped millions of people to improve their skills and achieve their goals. This new 'Coach' series of business books is created especially for people who want to focus proactively on a skill and to get a clear result at the end of it. Whereas many business books you walk the walk.

To my darling wife Caitlin – it's a privilege to share my life, truth and love with you. You are my partner, my best friend, my muse.

THE LEADERSHIP COACH

Tony Buon

First published in Great Britain in 2014 by Hodder & Stoughton. An Hachette UK company.

First published in US in 2014 by The McGraw-Hill Companies, Inc.

Copyright © Tony Buon 2014

British Library Cataloguing in Publication Data: a catalogue record for this title is available from the British Library.

Library of Congress Catalog Card Number: on file.

10 9 8 7 6 5 4 3 2 1

Paperback ISBN 978 1 473 601147

The publisher has used its best endeavours to ensure that any website addresses referred to in this book are correct and active at the time of going to press. However, the publisher and the author have no responsibility for the websites and can make no guarantee that a site will remain live or that the content will remain relevant, decent or appropriate.

The publisher has made every effort to mark as such all words which it believes to be trademarks. The publisher should also like to make it clear that the presence of a word in the book, whether marked or unmarked, in no way affects its legal status as a trademark.

Every reasonable effort has been made by the publisher to trace the copyright holders of material in this book. Any errors or omissions should be notified in writing to the publisher, who will endeavour to rectify the situation for any reprints and future editions.

Typeset by Cenveo® Publisher Services.

Printed and bound in Great Britain by CPI Group (UK) Ltd, Croydon CR0 4YY.

Hodder & Stoughton policy is to use papers that are natural, renewable and recyclable products and made from wood grown in sustainable forests. The logging and manufacturing processes are expected to conform to the environmental regulations of the country of origin.

Hodder & Stoughton Ltd
338 Euston Road
London NW1 3BH
www.hodder.co.uk

Also available in ebook

CONTENTS

MEET THE COACH

Tony Buon is a qualified workplace psychologist and behavioural scientist. He is a Certified Employee Assistance Professional (CEAP) and a Certified Mediator. Tony specializes in workplace leadership and communication and has more than 30 years' experience working with some of the world's leading organizations.

Tony holds graduate and postgraduate degrees in psychology, behavioural sciences and workplace education. His postgraduate research was into credentialism. Tony has taught Leadership, Psychology and Human Resources Management up to Master's Level in universities and colleges in Australia and the UK and has also taught on an accredited MBA programme in Scotland.

Born in Scotland, Tony spent many years in Australia where he owned and ran a large workplace consultancy with offices in 16 countries. He also opened one of the first private psychological services in the People's Republic of China. Tony today lives in the UK and travels widely throughout Europe, Africa and the Middle East delivering training programmes and seminars.

A small sample of Tony's past clients includes: 3M, Amnesty International, Atos, AXA, Coca-Cola, Diageo, DuPont, Halliburton, ICI, the London Hospital, Marathon Oil, McDonald's, Microsoft, NHS, Pfizer, the Royal Bank of Scotland, the Scottish Police College, Shell and the Sydney 2000 Olympic Games Organizing Committee.

Tony has also been interviewed in publications as diverse as *Rolling Stone* and *Reader's Digest*. He has appeared on CNN, the BBC, Trans-World Sport and many international television and radio stations.

HOW TO USE THIS BOOK

 OUTCOMES FROM THIS INTRODUCTION

- Know how to use this workbook effectively.
- Consider the problems of defining leadership.
- Evaluate your present leadership skills.

'As we look ahead into the next century, leaders will be those who empower others.'

Bill Gates, Former CEO, Microsoft, and philanthropist

Welcome to *The Leadership Coach*. This is not an academic textbook full of interesting but complex theories and ideas (though you will definitely find some interesting ideas). Neither is this a novel, so you don't need to start at the beginning and read every page in order. If there is a chapter that particularly interests you or is about something you're experiencing at the moment (such as conflict), then just skip to that chapter. This is, above all, a workbook – that is, a book containing instruction and exercises (called 'coaching sessions') relating to a particular subject, in this case leadership.

You will find the following features in each chapter:

 LEARNING OUTCOMES

Each chapter starts with three or four bullet points detailing the main outcomes of the chapter.

 COACHING SESSION

These include:

- workplace exercises using the discoveries made from completing a self-assessment
- illustrative charts and tables for you to complete
- checklists or tick lists
- forms and worksheets (for recording or challenging beliefs/thoughts)

- specific direction to achieve an outcome by studying other resources such as methodologies, bodies of knowledge, research papers and standards
- questions whose aim is to guide your learning.

 **COACH'S TIP**

The tips are key, 'snappy' pieces of advice, often drawn from the author's own experience.

 **ONLINE RESOURCE**

These boxes will contain complementary online resources and coaching sessions for you to download free of charge and make use of.

 **NEXT STEPS**

At the end of each chapter you will find a summary of what you have learned and what you have done in the chapter, as well as what comes next.

 **TAKEAWAYS**

At the end of each chapter, there are three or four questions to help you reflect on what you have learned from the chapter and carry that learning forward.

You can use this workbook in any way you like, but try to get it messy! Use lots of annotations, highlight stuff and complete the coaching sessions directly on the pages. Think of this as an 'active' book. Take a moment to look at the extra material we've made available for you online.

Most of all, however, use this workbook to develop your skills as a leader, no matter what type of leader you are and how much you already know.

 **COACH'S TIP**

A personal journey

When you decided to buy this book, you started on a personal journey of coaching. If you work through the material provided with an open and enquiring mind, you will become a better and more fulfilled leader.

░ COACHING SESSION 1

Why did you buy this workbook?

Now that you have read this far, we can assume you have purchased this workbook and have a reason for that purchase. Have a look at the possible reasons below and indicate which are correct for you. Tick all that apply to you.

I am new to leadership and I want to learn everything I can. ☐

I am an experienced leader – but I hope to learn some new things. ☑

I want to develop my skills as a leader. ☑

I have been promoted and I need to understand my new role. ☐

I liked the title. ☐

I need to understand twenty-first-century thinking on leadership. ☑

A friend/colleague/mentor recommended this book to me. ☐

Leadership is an area in which I need coaching. ☑

You can never learn too much – so I hope to get some tips on leadership. ☐

I try to read everything I can on this topic. ☐

I'm not sure. ☐

Other reasons (write them here):

_____

_____

_____

_____

_____

So now that you have started, take a few minutes to list all that you expect to learn from this workbook. What areas to you want to develop? Is there something in particular you want to learn about or a skill you particularly want to improve? Now complete Coaching session 2, before you do anything else in the workbook.

COACHING SESSION 2

What do you want to learn from this workbook?

_____

_____

_____

_____

_____

_____

_____

_____

_____

_____

_____

_____

_____

_____

_____

_____

_____

_____

Learning is a lifelong practice. Learning about leadership is also about learning about yourself. In the following chapters we will examine leadership in its various forms. We will look at leadership and management and see how they differ. We will look at how to handle conflict and how to manage your time. We will examine practical issues such as how to motivate others and how to lead a team. We will also look at some unique concerns for the twenty-first century, such as how to handle email and how to develop your emotional intelligence.

Once you have completed this introduction, take a moment to flick through all the following chapters. Remember: you do not have to complete this workbook in order, but, if you are new to leadership, it is a good idea to work through each chapter in turn and make sure that you take the time to complete all the coaching sessions.

WHAT IS LEADERSHIP?

This workbook is about leadership. But what is leadership?

The question 'What is a leader?' is actually a more complicated question than it first appears. There are many different definitions of a leader. At the most basic level, a leader is a person who leads or commands a group, team, organization or even a country. Some people say it's all about having the 'right' knowledge, skills and attitude. Possibly – but things are a little more complicated than that.

Great leaders develop through a never-ending process of self-study, self-reflection, education, training and experience. This workbook aims to help you improve as a leader. Warren Bennis is an American scholar and author, widely regarded as a pioneer of the contemporary field of leadership studies. He is quoted as saying: 'I used to think that running an organization was equivalent to conducting a symphony orchestra. But I don't think that's quite it; it's more like jazz. There is more improvisation.' He is no doubt correct, and in the modern business environment improvisation, or to use a current popular word, flexibility, is essential. Leadership is complicated and there are no 'one size fits all' solutions.

What are the benefits of being a leader? Given that 'the buck stops' with you, why would anyone want that responsibility? Why would you spend a lot of money and time studying leadership books or even spend years studying for an MBA?

Being a leader always comes with added responsibility in some form. It also comes with added pressures, added stress and added hours. So why would someone want to be a leader? Is it a need to be important or a need to make a difference?

There could be many reasons why you are in a leadership role. Possibly it's because it 'just happened'; possibly you were the only one who volunteered; perhaps you wanted the challenge. Later in this workbook we will look at the psychology of motivation and you may want to consider your personal motivation for being in a leadership role. The reasons why you are now working through this book are probably just as complicated as the question 'What is leadership?'

There are thousands of quotes about leadership, probably more than on any other subject. Here are several useful ones. What do you think?

> 'I must follow the people. Am I not their leader?'
>
> Benjamin Disraeli, British Prime Minister

> 'Lead me, follow me, or get out of my way.'
>
> General George Patton, US General in World War II

'Not the cry, but the flight of a wild duck, leads the flock to fly and follow.'

Chinese proverb

'Never doubt that a small group of thoughtful, concerned citizens can change the world. Indeed it is the only thing that ever has.'

Margaret Mead, cultural anthropologist

'Anyone can hold the helm when the sea is calm.'

Publilius Syrus, writer, 1st century BCE

'Arrogance diminishes wisdom.'

Arabic proverb

Leadership is about many things. It's about achieving tasks, giving unity to a group, meeting the needs of followers and achieving results. It's about understanding strategy and understanding oneself. It is about practical skills such as conflict management and philosophical concepts such as ethics and morals. It is about communication and understanding, strength and vision. Leadership is a journey and completing this workbook will be an important part of that journey.

COACHING SESSION 3

My definition of leadership

Have a go now at defining leadership. Try to keep this to fewer than 25 words if you can.

Getting things done. Enthusing the team to achieve the best results that can be achieved. Hanging in ther & staying the course, setting strategy & delivery -

Now have a look again at your definition and the quotes above. What is the same, what is different? How did you develop your idea of leadership?

Vision less prominent is conflict mgt.

More emphasis on determination (strength)

& unity (consensus?)

COACHING SESSION 4

Review of your leadership skills

Have a look at the list of leadership skills below and for each skill evaluate your competence, by ticking the corresponding box. Be as honest as you can. You will also find a link to where each skill is covered in this workbook if the term is new to you or if you want more information on a particular topic. There is also space to add any other skills you think of and evaluate your competence in them.

Skill	Evaluate your competence				Chapter link
Self-awareness	Excellent ☐	Good ☑	Average ☐	Needs Improvement ☐	3,7,10,11
People skills	Excellent ☐	Good ☐	Average ☑	Needs Improvement ☐	3,4,10,11
Empowering others	Excellent ☐	Good ☐	Average ☑	Needs Improvement ☐	2,11,13
Strategic planning	Excellent ☐	Good ☐	Average ☑	Needs Improvement ☑	1,6,9,12
Motivates others	Excellent ☐	Good ☐	Average ☑	Needs Improvement ☐	2,5,7
Self-motivation	Excellent ☐	Good ☐	Average ☑	Needs Improvement ☐	2,7,11
Creates vision	Excellent ☐	Good ☐	Average ☑	Needs Improvement ☑	1,6
Manages change	Excellent ☐	Good ☑	Average ☐	Needs Improvement ☐	2,6,8,9,12

Skill	Evaluate your competence				Chapter link
Emotional intelligence	Excellent ☐	Good ☐	Average ☑	Needs Improvement ☐	3,4,11
Builds teams	Excellent ☐	Good ☑	Average ☐	Needs Improvement ☐	2,5,7,10
Conflict management	Excellent ☐	Good ☐	Average ☐	Needs Improvement ☐	3,5,8,9
Active listening	Excellent ☐	Good ☐	Average ☐	Needs Improvement ☑	3,4,10
Makes decisions	Excellent ☐	Good ☑	Average ☐	Needs Improvement ☐	2,6,9,12
Delegates to others	Excellent ☐	Good ☐	Average ☐	Needs Improvement ☑	2,3,12
Manages time	Excellent ☐	Good ☐	Average ☐	Needs Improvement ☑	2,11,12
Goal setting	Excellent ☐	Good ☐	Average ☑	Needs Improvement ☐	2,7,13
Understands people	Excellent ☐	Good ☐	Average ☑	Needs Improvement ☐	1,3,10,11
Cross-cultural leadership	Excellent ☐	Good ☐	Average ☐	Needs Improvement ☐	3,4,10
Interpersonal skills	Excellent ☐	Good ☐	Average ☑	Needs Improvement ☐	3,4,11
Coaching and mentoring	Excellent ☐	Good ☐	Average ☑	Needs Improvement ☐	3,5,13
Drives results	Excellent ☐	Good ☑	Average ☐	Needs Improvement ☐	3,6,12
Communications	Excellent ☐	Good ☐	Average ☑	Needs Improvement ☐	
Presentations	Excellent ☐	Good ☐	Average ☐	Needs Improvement ☑	
	Excellent ☐	Good ☐	Average ☐	Needs Improvement ☐	

What areas do you excel in? What areas need improvement? Ask yourself this question: how would those who follow me rate me on each area?

Areas that need improvement : active listening, creating vision, delegation, time mgt & presenting.

Areas of strength enthusiasm, motivating others, driving results, building teams & decision-making

NEXT STEPS

The Harvard Business School Professor Rosabeth Moss Kantor said, 'Leaders are more powerful role models when they learn than when they teach.' You have started the process of learning. You have completed the Introduction. Now move on to the next chapter (or whichever chapter is attractive to you) and continue the learning process.

In the next chapter we will be looking at leadership theory (the interesting bits, of course!). Are leaders born or made? What are the characteristics of a good leader? We will look at the differences between leadership and management, and at the ideas of transformational and transactional leadership.

INTRODUCTION TO LEADERSHIP

 OUTCOMES FROM THIS CHAPTER

- Know the various theories and approaches to leadership study.
- Learn about transformational and transactional leadership theory.
- Understand the differences between leadership and management.

'Before you are a leader, success is all about growing yourself. When you become a leader, success is all about growing others.'

Jack Welch, former Chairman and CEO of General Electric

THEORY – BUT THE INTERESTING STUFF

The debate over whether great leaders are 'born' or whether they are 'made' has interested social scientists for centuries (and possibly no one else). This inevitably led to the search for the characteristics or traits of leaders. History's greatest philosophers have examined the question 'What characteristics distinguish a leader?' This was explored at length by ancient philosophers. Many styles of leadership were also evident in the Roman Republic and leadership was of great interest to Islamic scholars.

By the nineteenth century most writers concluded that leadership was inherited. In other words, leaders were born, not made. The so-called 'great man theory' of leadership became popular during this period and was based on a mythology of famous leaders such as Julius Caesar and Alexander the Great. The historian Thomas Carlyle had a significant impact on this philosophy of leadership. But many scholars also disagreed with this theory; in particular, the new sociologists suggested that leaders were products of society.

In the later parts of the nineteenth century through to the start of the twentieth century, psychology was becoming increasingly influential. This led to the focus on psychological and physical characteristics of traits of leaders.

This built on the 'great man' theories and suggested that people (normally men) born with characteristics such as 'height', 'self-assurance' and 'socio-economic status' were particularly suited to leadership. These even became selection criteria for leadership roles in the armed forces and even access to university study. Of course, you can probably see how much of this was somewhat self-fulfilling. If someone was from the ruling class, you would be seen as a 'natural' leader and you would have lots of confidence and have high socio-economic status.

⬚⬚ COACHING SESSION 5

Leadership traits?

Have a look at the following list and try to guess which ones have *not* been listed as leadership characteristics at some time by the 'trait theorists'.

Height	☐	Intelligence	☐
Class	☐	Extroversion	☐
Honesty	☐	Conscientiousness	☐
Masculinity	☐	Confidence	☐
Alertness	☐	Emotional stability	☐
Conservatism	☑	Tolerance	☐
Agreeableness	☑	Openness to experience	☐

All of these have been listed at some time by trait theorists. So, if particular characteristics are tied to leadership, then how do we explain people who possess these characteristics but are not leaders? This question is one of the further difficulties in using trait theories to explain leadership.

In the mid-twentieth century other theories emerged, including so-called 'situational theories' and 'behavioural theories'. **Situational theories** (also known as contingency theories) argued that people who are effective leaders in one situation may not be effective in other situations; leadership was therefore about the circumstances in which the person finds himself or herself. This group of theories says that no single psychological profile of a leader exists. Think of a well-respected leader – say Nelson Mandela, Oprah Winfrey or Mahatma Gandhi. Would they still be seen as great leaders if they had been born 20 years earlier or in a different country?

COACHING SESSION 6

Right place at the right time?

Can you think of examples of leaders you know who were in the right place at the right time? What was it about them and the situation that made them great?

List them here:

Strategist

Good communicator

Great judgement

Integrated with the zeitgest / jurisprudence

Cuts their cloth to the situation

Also in response to the criticisms of the trait approach, theorists began to consider leadership as a set of behaviours, evaluating the behaviour of successful leaders and identifying leadership styles. The principal assumption of these behavioural theories is that the skills of leadership can be acquired, developed and enhanced – therefore leaders are made and are not necessarily genetically predisposed to lead. This is the belief that great leaders are made, not born.

This was closely connected to the 'behaviourist' school of psychology founded by John B. Watson in 1913. These behaviourists believed that behaviours could be measured and that people could be trained to change their behaviour. The focus moved from leaders to leadership – and this became the dominant thinking into the 1950s and 1960s, which saw a boom in management training based on the idea that great leaders could be created with the 'correct' training or development.

CURRENT APPROACHES TO LEADERSHIP THEORY

Current approaches to leadership theory reflect the highly competitive and turbulent business environment by focusing on the most efficient use of people and how leaders can change and transform organizations. Although previous research on characteristics, behaviour and situational leadership are still relevant, leadership is increasingly being seen as an inspirational process. This has given rise to the terms 'transactional' and 'transformational' leadership.

Transactional and transformational leadership are often compared. The **transactional approach** is based on the leader having legitimate authority, for example the title of CEO or Captain. Transactional leaders are concerned with goals and outcomes, tasks, rewards and punishments. Such leadership is said to be more appropriate to stable environments and businesses. **Transformational leaders**, on the other hand, seek to motivate and gain the commitment of followers. This is achieved by sharing a vision, raising expectations and creating a feeling of trust so that followers will perform to a level exceeding their own expectations of what they had considered possible.

Most of the theories of leadership resurface in different forms, but they all have limitations. In a review of more than 300 scientific papers on leadership theory, Francis Yammarino from Binghamton University and his colleagues concluded that most studies in any of the areas of leadership research have not addressed issues appropriately in theory, data analysis, and inference drawing.

THE IMPORTANCE OF FOLLOWERS

Lao Tzu is an often-quoted ancient Chinese philosopher. His dates are disputed, as Chinese tradition places him as living in the sixth century BCE, where historians believe he was alive during the fourth century BCE. In this quote, we can see that he is suggesting that leadership is not about being the centre of attention, but about getting things done:

> *'To lead people, walk beside them [...]. As for the best leaders, the people do not notice their existence. The next best, the people honour and praise. The next, the people fear; and the next, the people hate [...]. When the best leader's work is done the people say, "We did it ourselves!"'*

And it is clear that you cannot be a leader without at least one follower (and preferably more). So any good definition of leadership must at least mention followers. Without followers there can be no leadership, as leadership is essentially a social phenomenon. The leader through their knowledge, personality, position or influence engages the followers in a common purpose and goal. The famous British Army officer Field Marshal Bernard Law Montgomery (Monty), who commanded the Eighth Army in World War II, said that his definition of leadership was:

> *'The capacity and the will to rally men and women to a common purpose and the character which inspires confidence.'*

MORE ABOUT TRANSFORMATIONAL LEADERSHIP

The most popular theory of leadership today is transformational leadership. The idea of transformational theory (also sometimes called **relationship theory**) is all about the close connections formed between a leader and their followers. Transformational leaders motivate and inspire people through their vision and high ethical and moral standards.

Research suggests that organizations led by transformational leaders have higher levels of performance than those led by other types of leaders. Transformational leaders' high expectations give their subordinates the self-confidence to persist in the face of setbacks, often resulting in exceptional performance. Executives described as transformational leaders pay attention to their followers' personal interests, express confidence in their abilities, and share a vision that is clear and engaging to all.

The concept of transformational leadership was initially introduced by leadership expert and American presidential biographer James MacGregor Burns. Researcher Bernard Bass expanded upon Burns' original ideas to develop what is often referred to as Bass's Transformational Leadership Theory. Bass described four factors of transformational leadership. This can be seen in Figure 1.1 below.

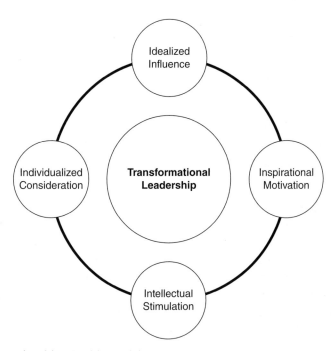

Figure 1.1 Transformational Leadership model

1. **Intellectual Stimulation**   Leaders not only challenge the status quo; they also encourage this in followers.

2. **Individualized Consideration**   The leader acts as a mentor or coach to the follower and listens to the follower's concerns and meets their needs.

3. **Inspirational Motivation**   Leaders have a clear vision that they are able to articulate to followers.

4. **Idealized Influence**   Followers trust and respect the leader so they emulate and internalize the leader's values and beliefs.

Transformational leaders can come in various forms. But what they have in common is that they:

- enhance their followers' self-esteem
- display high levels of ethical behaviour
- empower others
- increase commitment and loyalty
- act as a positive role model
- motivate others
- communicate effectively
- stimulate creativity
- challenge the status quo
- embrace change
- develop others through coaching and mentoring.

MORE ABOUT TRANSACTIONAL LEADERSHIP

Transactional leadership style can be contrasted with transformational styles. Transactional leadership is all about 'you scratch my back and I'll scratch yours'. Transactional leadership is concerned with maintaining the normal flow of operations. Transactional leaders use disciplinary power and an array of incentives to motivate employees to perform. The term 'transactional' refers to the fact that this type of leader essentially motivates subordinates by exchanging rewards for performance.

A transactional leader usually does not look ahead; instead, transactional managers are concerned with making sure that everything operates smoothly today. Rules, procedures and standards are essential in transactional leadership.

While transactional leadership can be effective in some situations, it is usually not as effective as transformational leadership, particularly when it comes to followers achieving their full potential.

COACHING SESSION 7

Transformational leadership

Think of a leader whom you would categorize as transformational. Write down their name and then list the qualities (both personal and professional) they have/had.

Name of transformational leader:	
Qualities (personal)	Qualities (professional)

⛁ COACHING SESSION 8

Are you a transformational leader?

Do you have transformational leadership qualities? Here are various statements related to transformational leadership. Read each statement and indicate whether you agree or disagree with it. Be as honest as you can when answering – remember that this is how you presently are, not how you want to be.

STATEMENT	Agree	Disagree
Inspiring others has always come easy to me.		
I am a good delegator.		
I see change as a good idea.		
I enjoy coaching or mentoring others.		
I would not ask a follower to do something that I wouldn't do myself.		
Making people feel good about themselves is important to me.		
Doing good is more important than doing what works.		
Sharing power is important.		
My followers often 'go the extra mile' for me.		
Loyalty is more important than efficiency.		
Creativity and innovation are the keys to success.		
Listening is more important than talking.		
I take time to learn what people need from me so that they can be successful.		
I have a clear vision of the future.		
I give my followers independence to work towards a goal as they see fit.		
I try to intellectually challenge my followers.		

STATEMENT	Agree	Disagree
I believe that it is vitally important to be a good role model.		
Empowering followers will result in greater long-term results.		
I am genuinely positive and enthusiastic.		
I ask others for their thoughts and perspectives.		
Total score		

Results

A score of more 'agrees' than 'disagrees' (>11) means that you are more inclined towards transformational leadership. A score above 15 agrees shows very strong transformational views. You are well placed to become an effective leader in today's business world.

If you scored more 'disagrees' than 'agrees' (>11), then your views are more in line with the transactional approach. A score of above 15 disagrees shows little support for transformational ideas and is more consistent with transactional management. Transactional leaders are necessary to the day-to-day operations of the business. Transactional leaders focus on clarifying employee's roles and providing rewards contingent on performance.

IS LEADERSHIP THE SAME AS MANAGEMENT?

There is a continuing debate about the difference between leadership and management. While leadership and management are closely linked and even connected, there are significant differences. Not all managers are leaders and not all leaders can manage. Often it is wrongly assumed that anyone in a management position is a leader. Leadership is performed by people who are not in management positions (for example an informal team leader).

Some writers argue that, although management and leadership overlap, the two activities are not the same. The degree of overlap is a point of disagreement but it does appear that leadership and management entail a unique set of activities or functions. In his 2007 book *Leaders: The Strategies for Taking Charge*, Warren Bennis cogently said that: 'Managers do things right, while leaders do the right things.' Apple Inc. co-founder Steve Jobs revolutionized multiple industries with his innovative products but he was not the world's greatest manager, according to biographer Walter Isaacson. However, he surrounded himself with top talent and great managers. That is really smart leadership.

COACHING SESSION 9

Leaders and managers

So what do you think? Make a list below of all the things you think a leader does and then all the things a manager does. Use your own experiences here either as a follower or a leader (or even as a manager).

Leader	Manager

Here is a list based on what the experts say. How does it compare to yours? Did you add anything or did you miss anything?

Leader	Manager
Does the right things	Does things right
Transformational	Transactional
Establishes vision	Plans and budgets
Develops strategy	Develops policies and procedures
Develops plans	Monitors results against plan
Communicates vision and strategy	Communicates policy and rules
Motivates and inspires	Produces order and consistency
Is mostly concerned with people	Is mostly concerned with assets
Finds resources and funding	Manages resources and funds
Identifies problems and obstacles	Problem solves
Influences creation of teams	Manages teams
Aligns people	Organizes and staffs
Is focused outwards	Is focused inwards
Takes risks	Manages risk or avoids risks
Empowers others	Controls and manages others
Is concerned with influence	Is concerned with authority
Uses conflict	Avoids conflict
Challenges the status quo	Accepts the status quo
Produces positive/dramatic change	Manages and monitors change
Sees the forest	Sees the trees

We can see that management and leadership are not the same thing. But both are necessary. Organizations give people the legitimate authority to lead, but there is no guarantee that they will be able to lead well.

 COACH'S TIP

Strong leadership, strong management

Organizations need both strong leadership and strong management to be truly efficient. In today's ever-changing workplace, we need leaders who inspire and transform. But we also need managers to ensure a smoothly functioning workplace.

So what role are you more suited for, leadership or management?

COACHING SESSION 10

Your preferred role

For each statement, tick the column that best describes you. Please answer questions according to how you actually are (rather than how you think you should be), and don't worry if some questions seem to score in the 'wrong direction'. When you are finished, total up your scores and read the interpretation box to see what the score means.

STATEMENT	Not at all	Rarely	Some times	Often	Very often
I like to be at the front in most situations.	1	2	3	4	5
I am interested in strategy.	1	2	3	4	5
I use conflict to achieve my goals.	1	2	3	4	5
I am a 'glass half-empty' kind of person.	5	4	3	2	1
I am better at identifying problems than solving them.	1	2	3	4	5
I would rather do than observe.	1	2	3	4	5
Interpersonal communication bores me.	5	4	3	2	1
People interest me.	1	2	3	4	5
I see myself as a good manager rather than a good leader.	5	4	3	2	1
I love change – it energizes me.	1	2	3	4	5
I like to overcome barriers or avoid them.	5	4	3	2	1
Learning new things excites me.	1	2	3	4	5
I take many risks.	1	2	3	4	5
I would rather develop a plan than monitor it.	1	2	3	4	5
I avoid speaking in most meetings if I can.	5	4	3	2	1
Score					
Total score					

Score interpretation

Score	Comment
15–34	Management is your passion. You are probably best suited to being in a management rather than in a leadership role. This does not mean you can't lead or that this workbook is not for you. By completing this workbook, you will strengthen your management and leadership skills. This is especially important if you find yourself leading rather than managing others in the future.
35–55	This would show that you are interested pretty equally in both leadership and management. It is not yet clear which role you would be most suited for. By working through this workbook, you may find that the answer becomes clearer.
56–75	You are a leader. It is clear that from this result that leadership is your passion. You are probably best suited in a leadership rather than a management role. Work through all the following chapters to develop your leadership skills.

TYPES OF LEADER

Leadership comes in many forms. We have leaders in nearly every social situation that involves groups, both acknowledged and not. Leaders can be of any gender, age, religion or disposition. They can be loved, hated or both (sometimes at the same time).

Leadership takes place on many levels. The following model (Figure 1.2) involves four levels. These are:

1. Self
2. Team
3. Functional
4. Strategic

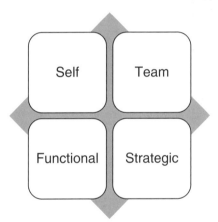

Figure 1.2 The four levels of leadership

- **Self-leadership** is the modern version of Socrates' instruction to 'know thyself'. Self-leadership is the foundation for all leadership. Simply put, if you don't or can't lead yourself, what business do you have leading others? We will explore this area in detail when we look at emotional intelligence (EI). It was the psychologist Daniel Goleman who first introduced EI to a wide audience with his 1995 book of that name. Goleman has said that self-awareness is the 'keystone' of EI (see Chapter 11).

- **Team or group leadership** (effectively a team is a particular type of group) is where someone is a leader of a team of approximately four to twenty people. Meredith Belbin, the British researcher and team theorist, argues that the optimum size for a team is four to six people. Do you agree?

- **Functional or operational leadership** is where a leader is leading a key part of an organization, usually with several team leaders under their control. We could describe this leader as a 'leader of leaders'.

- **Strategic leadership** is about leading the whole organization. This kind of leadership sets the direction for the growth and success of the organization. It is about vision, mission and transformation. Under the strategic leader(s) are the functional leaders.

→ NEXT STEPS

We have seen that leadership involves a set of critical skills, knowledge and attitudes. You are not born a leader, you become one, at least in part because your followers let you. We have also seen that management and leadership are different but interconnected approaches. But what are they? This question has been explored by many writers and scholars.

Managers at any level cannot be seen as purely functional and hierarchical members of an organization. They require excellent technical and professional skills but sometimes they lack necessary leadership skills. This is common in many technical organizations where a very competent engineer, for example, is steadily promoted higher in the organization and where increasingly it is his or her leadership skills that are lacking. It is interesting to note that today a majority of those going back to university to study MBAs and other leadership programmes are professionals who realize that, while they have excellent technical or professional skills, they lack fundamental leadership skills. The US President J.F. Kennedy is reported to have said: 'Leadership and learning are indispensable to each other…' He was certainly right. This workbook has been designed to help you grow as a leader – to help you learn and improve your leadership skills.

In the next chapter we will look at time management and delegation. Managing time is an essential skill for any leader and this chapter will provide you with some excellent tips and strategies to better manage your time. We will also be looking at delegation and seeing how this valuable skill can both free you up for your core activities and enhance the role of others.

TAKEAWAYS

Are leaders born or made? What do you base your answer on?

_____

_____

_____

_____

_____

_____

_____

_____

_____

_____

_____

_____

_____

Can you describe transformational and transactional leadership? How do they differ?

_____

_____

_____

_____

_____

_____

_____

_____

_____

_____

_____

_____

_____

What is the difference between leadership and management? Which do you prefer?

_____

_____

_____

_____

_____

_____

_____

_____

_____

_____

TIME MANAGEMENT AND DELEGATION

 OUTCOMES FROM THIS CHAPTER

- Learn how to improve your time management.
- Acquire ways to improve your use of email.
- Understand the importance of maintaining a work–life balance.
- Understand the importance of delegation.

'Keeping time, time, time
In a sort of Runic rhyme,
To the tintinnabulation that so musically wells,
From the bells, bells, bells.'

Edgar Allan Poe, American poet

SO WHAT IS TIME?

The question 'What is time?' is surprisingly difficult to answer. Most of the answers are related to physics, quantum mechanics and the 24-hour clock. Modern atomic clocks are the most accurate timekeepers known and are based on the oscillation between the nucleus of an atom and the surrounding electrons. Science writer John Gribbin states in his 1996 book *Companion to the Cosmos* that everybody knows what time is, but nobody can explain what it is. And even the concept of 'managing time' has its problems, for we can't actually *manage* time. It's a constant and we have no control over it. But it does provide us with a reference system in which events can be ordered from the past through the present into the future.

COACHING SESSION 11

Your definition of time

Have a go yourself at defining time. Imagine that you are answering a young child's question: 'What is time?' How would you respond?

_____

_____

_____

_____

_____

_____

_____

_____

Time management in the area of leadership is big business and most leaders will have read or attended training courses on time management. We are often told that people who use time-management techniques are the highest achievers in all walks of life, the suggestion being that, if you use these skills, then you will be successful. If only it were that easy. Being in control of your time is a real skill and clearly some people are better at it than others.

The late American writer and educator Stephen Covey provided a useful classification scheme for the different time-management approaches a leader can use (Covey 1994):

- **First generation:** reminders based on clocks and watches (nowadays add smartphones).

- **Second generation:** planning and goal setting based on a diary system.

- **Third generation:** planning, prioritizing, controlling activities on a daily basis.

- **Fourth generation:** being efficient and proactive using any of the above tools.

Clearly, most leaders should be at the fourth level. A leader needs to understand and apply the often-quoted statement: 'Concentrate on results, not on being busy.' Many people fill up their day with work but achieve little. This is because they are not focusing on the right things. Most leaders simply spend too much time on 'time-wasters'.

COACHING SESSION 12

Time-wasters

Complete the table below and indicate which of the time-wasters apply to you and why. Also consider what you could do about it.

Time-wasters at work	Is this me?	Why and what could I do about it?
Getting interrupted by other people	Always Sometimes Never	
Interrupting other people for a chat	Always Sometimes Never	
Over-reliance on email	Always Sometimes Never	
Trying to do more than one thing at once	Always Sometimes Never	
Running or attending pointless meetings	Always Sometimes Never	
Liking to help others or always saying 'yes'	Always Sometimes Never	
'Surf the web' breaks	Always Sometimes Never	

Instant messaging, social media, etc.	Always Sometimes Never	
Accepting unrealistic deadlines	Always Sometimes Never	
Getting easily distracted	Always Sometimes Never	
Forgetting to do things	Always Sometimes Never	
Having trouble saying 'no'	Always Sometimes Never	
Not filing documents or emails regularly	Always Sometimes Never	
Computer games	Always Sometimes Never	
Losing old emails	Always Sometimes Never	
Having an untidy desk	Always Sometimes Never	

If you said 'Always' or 'Sometimes' to anything above, pick one item a week to work on and eliminate. This may take a while – but it will be worth it.

COACH'S TIP

How do you spend your time?

If you want to manage your time efficiently, probably the most important thing you can do is keep a detailed diary of how you spend your time for a week or two. Split your day into 30-minute blocks and record exactly how you spend your time. After one or two weeks, carefully analyse the results. You will probably be surprised at how much of your time is 'unproductive'.

COACHING SESSION 13

Time log

Working on 30-minute intervals, record how you spend your time. Have a look at the example below to get an idea of how to do this. If your working week is pretty regular then you only need to do this for one week. If an average week is very varied for you, then you will probably need to do this for two weeks to get a proper picture of how you spend your time. You can complete this in an existing diary (paper or electronic) or use a time-log sheet as below.

Time	Day: Monday	Time	Day: Monday
8:30	Drove to work - listened to radio	1:30	Organized my desk and sorted my files
9:00	Read and replied to email	2:00	Had coffee and chat with Bill - also more email
9:30	Read report and chatted with Sue about TV show	2:30	Made 2 phone calls and arranged one meeting
10:00	Regular Monday meeting - started 10 mins late	3:00	Started to write ACME report
10:30	Meeting overran - then went for good coffee	3:30	Coffee break and continued on ACME report
11:00	Read more emails - spent 10 minutes surfing web	4:00	Discussed ACME with Simon and Sue
11:30	Phoned IT department about new monitor	4:30	Personal calls and more coffee
12:00	Worked on plan for ACME report	5:00	Checked emails and sorted out computer problem
12:30	Went to lunch - long line had to wait	5:30	Organized what I would do tomorrow on ACME
1:00	Finished lunch and met with Simon	6:00	Drove home - bad traffic as usual - home at 6:45

ONLINE RESOURCE

You can download a time-log template by going to this link:

www.TYCoachbooks.com/Leadership

MANAGING YOUR TIME WELL

'What is important is seldom urgent and what is urgent is seldom important.'

Dwight D. Eisenhower

One very useful tool for managing your time is the Eisenhower Method. This method is named after US President Dwight D. Eisenhower and was popularized by Stephen Covey in his 1994 bestselling book *First Things First.* This tool provides a simple but powerful organizing process that helps you categorize tasks so that you focus on what is results driven, not merely what makes you busy. In this method, tasks are divided into four quadrants as follows:

1. Important and Urgent (emergencies, deadlines, problems, crises, commitments, etc.) **'Do It Now'**	**2. Important, Not Urgent** (self-and staff development, projects, meetings, recreation, etc.) **'Plan It'**
3. Urgent, Not Important (interruptions, some meetings, some email, routine tasks, etc.) **'Delegate It'**	**4. Not Urgent, Not Important** (time-wasters, junk mail, trivia, busy-work, some meetings, etc.) **'Bin It'**

Most leaders spend most of their time in quadrants 1, 3 and 4, while quadrant 2 is where you should plan most of your day. Quadrant 3 is where quality leadership happens.

COACHING SESSION 14

Use the Eisenhower Method

Using the template below, make a list of all the things you did yesterday (yes, *everything*) and see which quadrant each thing would fit.

1. Important and Urgent (emergencies, deadlines, problems, crisis, commitments, time-due projects, firefighting)	2. Important, Not Urgent (self-and team development, projects, meetings, recreation, networking, learning, training)
'Do it now'	*'Plan it'*
3. Urgent, Not Important (interruptions, some meetings, some email, routine tasks, some calls, false deadlines)	4. Not Urgent, Not Important (time-wasters, junk mail, trivia, busy-work, some meetings, some calls, some social media)
'Delegate it'	*'Bin it'*

Which quadrant is the most full?

_____

Are you spending too much time in certain quadrants? If so, why do you think this is?

_____

_____

_____

_____

Most activities should be in quadrant 2. If they are not, why do you think this is?

_____

_____

_____

_____

_____

 ONLINE RESOURCE

You can download the template of the Eisenhower Method by going to this link:

www.TYCoachbooks.com/Leadership

MANAGING YOUR EMAIL

Since the 1990s email has eclipsed paper-based mail and fax to become the standard in the business world, and although social media and instant messaging are closing in (particularly with younger people), email still holds firm in the business arena.

Email might be a great communication tool but, if you're not careful, it can eat up your valuable time. Many leaders spend an hour or more every day processing email. This is usually wasted time, time you can reclaim if you learn the basics of managing your email.

You should view handling your email as a time-management skill that you need to improve. Email can create a sense of urgency, but most of the messages you receive are not urgent. Controlling the volume of messages you receive is not always possible, but you can learn to use email more efficiently.

> 'It is exhausting knowing that most of the time the phone rings, most of the time there's an email, most of the time there's a letter, someone wants something of you.'
>
> Stephen Fry, author, actor and tweeter

So how are you at managing your email? Do you have good email time-management skills? Take the following test and see. After you get your score, why not give the test to a few friends or colleagues and see how they score?

COACHING SESSION 15

Assess your email ability

Complete the following quiz as honestly as you can. Remember to answer questions according to how you really are – not how you wish to be.

Question	Never	Sometimes	Frequently	Always
I only check email at certain times of the day	1	2	3	4
My email inbox is cluttered	4	3	2	1
I store email messages in folders to read them later	1	2	3	4
I keep emails brief and to the point.	1	2	3	4
I open email as soon as it arrives.	4	3	2	1
I prioritize my email and deal with it using time management.	1	2	3	4
I perform housekeeping on my email files and do backups.	1	2	3	4
I have a 'pending' folder for emails that need a lot of time.	1	2	3	4
I email when I should phone or write.	4	3	2	1
Subject lines on my email are clear and concise.	1	2	3	4
I ignore spelling, grammar and punctuation rules in emails.	4	3	2	1
Wherever possible I concentrate on one subject per message.	1	2	3	4
I respond to emails within 24 hours.	1	2	3	4
I have email spam software on all my devices and computers.	1	2	3	4
I avoid using bcc and cc unnecessarily.	1	2	3	4
I have email signatures on all my devices.	1	2	3	4
I avoid using email for private and confidential matters.	1	2	3	4

Question	Never	Sometimes	Frequently	Always
I think about the tone in my emails before I send them.	1	2	3	4
I respond in anger to emails that upset me.	4	3	2	1
I always think before I click.	1	2	3	4
Score				
Total score				

Score interpretation

Score	Comment
20–45	You need to learn to use email more efficiently and reduce time wasted and errors made. You need to work on your email communication skills. Use the list above to help you.
46–65	You have reasonable to good email management skills, but they could improve. Highlight the areas where you are weak above and work on them.
66–80	You use email efficiently; well done. Keep looking for new ways to further streamline your practices and increase your efficiency even more.

 ONLINE RESOURCE

You can download a copy of this quiz by going to:

www.TYCoachbooks.com/Leadership

IMPROVING YOUR USE OF EMAIL

To improve your email time management, try to apply the following ten tips:

Tip 1: Know your audience

Make sure that you know your audience: if they rarely use email, a letter or phone call may be a better method of communication. Also, don't use email as an excuse to avoid talking to someone or to avoid an uncomfortable situation. Use the phone, especially for complex issues, emotional discussions and sensitive discussions.

Tip 2: Get the tone right

Emails should be informal, but professional. Your email message reflects you and your organization, so traditional spelling, grammar and punctuation rules apply.

Avoid slang (LOL, cool, etc.) and shortened words (4u, gr8, k). Also don't use a strange font. Verdana or Calibri are good professional fonts but Comic Sans is not.

Do not use email for messages that can be easily misinterpreted. As an email does not have a tone of voice or body language, people often question what an email actually means. And the solution is not emoticons – these 'cute' smiley faces have no place in a professional email.

Tip 3: Keep it brief

Keep your messages brief and to the point. If you have a lot to say, send a memo or letter, or use an attachment. Make sure the subject line relates to the email content. Try to focus on one topic per email message whenever possible.

It is also important to remember not to keep people waiting for a response. Answer as quickly as possible. A good time-management rule to use for a standard response is to always respond within 24 business hours.

Tip 4: Check your email at set times during the day

This tip worries a lot of people, but it is very efficient. Check your email at set times during the day. Do not have your email software open all the time and in view. You will have increased productivity and efficiency if you check and respond to email only at set times each day (say 10 a.m., 1 p.m. and 5 p.m. on weekdays). You can make this twice a day or even hourly depending on your role and responsibilities. Remember: if it is really urgent, people will call you or get in touch some other way.

Tip 5: Have a strategy

Have a strategy in place for how you will handle email when you do check it at set times during the day. For example, as you open each email, do the following:

- If it requires a quick response (one or two minutes), respond to it and delete (or file) it.
- If it requires a response but is not the best use of your time, try to think of a way of forwarding (delegating) it.
- If it is going to take time to respond (beyond a minute or two) to, schedule it for action in your diary and then move it to a 'pending' folder.

Tip 6: Manage your inbox

Do not leave mail in the 'inbox' folder. Make sure you clear out your email inbox whenever you check your email. Remember: a cluttered email inbox is as bad as a cluttered desk. A cluttered inbox will mean that you will find it difficult to find anything. Declutter your inbox by setting up folders in your email software. This is very easy in Outlook and Gmail.

Tip 7: Restrict bcc & cc usage

Don't use bcc to keep others from seeing whom you have copied in. Be cautious with your use of cc; overuse simply clutters other people's inboxes. If you want less email – send less email.

It is always worth checking that you're sending it to the right people, and that you haven't cc'd in anyone inappropriate. A good tip is to enter the recipient's email address last.

Tip 8: Use a signature

Use an email signature that includes contact information, including your mailing address and telephone numbers, so that people know who you are. But keep it professional and short.

You can also use signatures as a form of auto-text to save typing time. For example, if you often write something like:

> 'Thank you for your enquiry about employment in our company. I have attached the relevant forms and a link to our HR website. I look forward to receiving your application in due course.'

...don't type it out each time; save the text as a 'signature' and simple select that signature each time you need to give this response. You can also achieve the same result using third-party apps.

Tip 9: Think about privacy

Remember that email isn't private. Don't send confidential/private information via email. Don't use email for anything that will reflect badly on you or your organization. Remember that anything you send can be forwarded, saved and printed by people it was never intended for. Don't use email for anything obscene, libellous, offensive or racist. Think of a business email as a binding contract.

Tip 10: Think before you click

Never send an email when you are angry or upset. Step away from the computer and cool down. Ask yourself whether you would say this to the person if you were face to face. Never try responding to emails when you have just woken up or are under the influence of alcohol or other drugs. Think before you click the send button.

COACH'S TIP

The email golden rule

Remember to type unto others as you would have them type unto you.

DELEGATION

Whether we are a delegator or a delegatee, the ability to get things done through others is essential for good leadership. Understanding a few basic concepts can make the process easier.

The purpose of delegation is twofold:

- It gives you more time to concentrate on important things.
- It develops and motivates your people.

When you delegate, you make use of other people's specialist skills and this can save time and energy by utilizing concurrent activity. Delegation can be not only downwards; it can be sideways or even upwards.

Many leaders fail to delegate because they are unable or unwilling to let go or because they have a lack of faith in other people's abilities. Of course, some leaders are scared that the delegatee will perform better than them. You may have other reasons for your lack of delegation, such as:

- liking to give an impression of being overworked and busy
- believing you can do it more quickly or better yourself
- enjoying doing the work – 'getting your hands dirty'
- difficult or aggressive subordinates who resist delegation.

When you delegate, you should if possible delegate entire jobs; this provides the delegatee with a sense of achievement. It is worth considering delegating routine tasks that you regularly perform or jobs that others can do better and possibly for less cost. Of course, the Eisenhower Method applies here. You can usually delegate 'Category 3: Urgent, not important' tasks.

THE DELEGATION CONTINUUM

In the last two chapters we have seen how many leadership theorists give different definitions of leadership styles. In 1973 Tannenbaum and Schmidt came up with a range of leadership behaviours, ranging from leader-centred (task) to subordinate-centred (relationship). This is usually shown as a simple illustration, as shown in Figure 2.1.

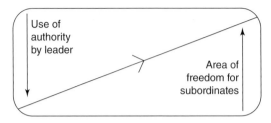

Figure 2.1 The Delegation Continuum (adapted from Tannenbaum and Schmidt 1973)

This model suggests that the leader should, through the use of sound delegation, aim to take the subordinate from one end to the other, up the scale. This is also consistent with the process of succession planning, something every leader should be considering. This kind of delegation can take some time and it is necessary to explain what you're doing and provide ongoing coaching.

The Tannenbaum and Schmidt model shows the relationship between the levels of freedom that a leader chooses to give and the level of authority used by the manager. Tannenbaum and Schmidt emphasized the importance of delegation and freedom in decision making. As the subordinate's freedom increases, the leader's authority decreases, and this is a good thing for both.

When you do delegate, try also to delegate responsibility and the authority to make decisions. But don't try to delegate unpleasant tasks which are really your responsibility or new tasks without giving coaching or training.

🗣🗣 COACHING SESSION 16

Delegation

First: list all the tasks or activities you are presently doing yourself that could be performed satisfactorily by someone else. Try to be really honest here and don't focus on whom you could delegate to – focus instead on the tasks or activities you presently perform that someone else could do for lower cost or better.

1
2

3

4

5

6

Second: look at the list of tasks or activities above. Choose three and move them into the next table. Ask yourself: 'Why don't I presently delegate these tasks or activities?'

Task or activity	Why don't I presently delegate this?
1	
2	
3	

Third: Select one of the tasks or activities from the above table that you could delegate to someone else. Complete the next table for that task or activity. Ask yourself what you need to do to ensure that the task or activity is delegated correctly. For example, enquire:

- Does the person require coaching or training?

- Is this a task that they might find stretching and rewarding (even though you don't)?

- Am I delegating a whole job?

- Can I delegate responsibility and the authority to make decisions?

Task or activity:

I will delegate this task to (name):

Necessary actions are:

I will delegate this on (insert date):

Your last step is actually to delegate an activity or task to the real person you have named above. But before you do, follow the 'Seven delegation steps' below.

THE SEVEN DELEGATION STEPS

When you choose to delegate, it is essential to follow the right steps. This model should help you do this effectively and efficiently. The model, also called the commitment cycle, can be seen in Figure 2.2 and is explained fully below.

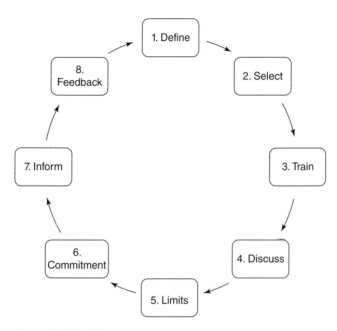

Figure 2.2 The seven steps to delegation

The commitment cycle

1. **Define:** Make sure that you can define the task or job you are going to delegate. Is it a 'whole' or 'part' job (aim for 'whole')? Are there clear competencies attached? Ask yourself: 'Is this a task or responsibility that should be delegated?'

2. **Select:** Decide which person or team you will delegate to. What is in it for them? Are they available and do they have the time? Try to make it a 'stretch' goal for the delegatee.

3. **Train:** Assess the training needs of the delegatee. Do they understand what needs to be done? How much instruction/coaching or mentoring is needed? Get your timing right here.

4. **Discuss:** Take the time to explain to the delegatee why you are delegating this task or responsibility. Clearly explain the reasons for the delegation. Encourage questions and listen actively to what the delegatee has to say.

5. **Limits:** State the boundaries, parameters and responsibilities involved. Explain budgets or approval levels. Agree on clear review dates and what the delegatee should do if they experience difficulties.

6. **Commitment:** Confirm that the delegatee accepts the delegation and do not assume that they have accepted the tasks or work without verbal consent (in some cases you could even need written approval, though that would be unusual). Now let go. Let the person attempt the task or work without you 'micro-managing'.

7. **Inform:** Make sure that you tell anyone else involved about the delegation. Decide who else needs to know and tell them yourself; don't leave it to the delegatee. This could be team members, other managers or clients. This also has the benefit of sending a clear message that the task or job is no longer your responsibility.

8. **Feedback:** This should be ongoing, not just at the conclusion. Make sure that you let the delegatee know how they are getting along and about any areas that need improvement. Remain available to the delegatee, particularly in the early stages. Also, take some time to reflect on and evaluate your own delegation behaviour. Could you have done something better? Did it save you time?

9. Delegation is an obvious way of releasing more time. Delegation is not a quick fix but it is an astute long-term investment. If you practise delegation, you will become better at it and you will find it one of your most valuable leadership tools.

→ NEXT STEPS

In this chapter we have looked at time management and delegation. While the question of what time actually is is a challenging one with many answers, we have seen that time provides us with a reference system in which events can be ordered from the past through the present into the future. Essential to time management is a change in focus, a change from being 'busy' to a focus on outcomes. Finally, we looked at delegation and why it is an important skill for any leader.

In the next chapter we will look at communication skills. You will see that many of the problems experienced in organizations are due to communication problems. Communication is the exchange and flow of information and ideas from one person to another. It sounds simple, but there can be many barriers and these barriers can cause communication problems. We will also look at body language and active listening.

TAKEAWAYS

List **five** things you presently waste time on and want to change:

1 _____

_____

2 _____

_____

3 _____

_____

4 _____

_____

5 _____

_____

Email is a great communication tool, but it can be a huge 'time thief'. How could you improve your email usage?

_____

_____

_____

_____

Why is delegation vital to a leader?

COMMUNICATION SKILLS

3

OUTCOMES FROM THIS CHAPTER

- Understand that many of the difficulties experienced in organizations are due to communication problems.
- Learn about non-verbal communication and some of the common myths about 'body language'.
- Learn how to improve your listening skills.

'The problem in the world today is communication ... too much communication!'

Homer Simpson, *The Simpsons*

In this chapter we will look at the complex area of human communication. Many of the problems that occur in organizations are the direct result of people failing to communicate. A lack of communication skills, particularly with leaders, is central to most problems. Almost any 'people problem' faced by the leader can be traced back to bad communication and probably the fact that someone is not listening.

Poor communication leads to confusion, anger and distrust and can cause a sound strategic plan to fail. Good communication leads to clarity, openness, success and respect of the leader. In all the surveys done about what people want in the leaders, the ability to communicate well is always a top result.

CASE STUDY: SARAH

Consider the example of Sarah, a recently appointed CEO in a mid-size organization. Keen to give a good impression, Sarah arrived early each day and got straight to work, often not leaving until late in the evening. While she felt a bit overwhelmed with the amount of paperwork and the financial issues she had found, she was energized by the difficulties of turning a failing business around. She was sure that her team was behind her. Of course they must be – she was working so hard to protect all their jobs!

However, feedback from her management team was contradictory on this. They indicated that many staff saw her as 'aloof' and 'arrogant'. Sarah was shocked. How could they have got her so wrong? One of the experienced managers from HR hesitated then suggested to her that she should look at how she communicated with the team. For instance, when she arrived early and rushed to her office, did she take time to stop and chat to people? Did she ever visit the cafeteria and join in with the discussions on the tables? Did she even know that the department volleyball team had just got into the finals of the local lunchtime league?

Sarah thought: 'I've not got time to chat when I'm trying to turn this business around. I don't have time for lunch, never mind talking about volleyball!'

COACHING SESSION 17

Case study: reflection

What do you think Sarah should do?

_____

_____

_____

_____

_____

_____

_____

After the meeting, however, Sarah reflected that the HR Manager might be on to something. So for the next couple of weeks she promised herself that she would take a few minutes when she arrived to chat with the receptionists, walk to her office and stop at a couple of desks, take 30 minutes to have a bite in the canteen with others and not eat at her desk. She even went to one of the lunchtime games to cheer on the team.

At the next management meeting she was amazed with the answers from her team. 'We've had so much excellent feedback from staff about you,' said one manager. 'Yes,' said another, 'people are saying that you are so approachable and they are confident that you'll turn the business around.' Sarah nodded to the HR Manager and said, 'Yes, communication is so important – if you get that wrong, nothing else will work either.'

In this case study we can see how just doing your job well is not enough for a leader. People expect and want to be heard, to be communicated with on an emotional level and to see their leaders as approachable and human. Get it right and communication is a fantastic tool, but get it wrong and the costs can be enormous – for you and your organization.

SO WHAT IS COMMUNICATION?

'The single biggest problem in communication is the illusion that it has taken place.'

George Bernard Shaw, Irish playwright

Communication is the exchange and flow of information and ideas from one person to another. It involves a sender transmitting an idea to a receiver. Effective communication occurs only if the receiver understands the exact information or idea that the sender intended to transmit.

Studying the communication process is essential because you coach, co-ordinate, counsel, direct, evaluate and supervise through this process. It is a necessary part of your competency as a leader.

What is involved in the communication process?

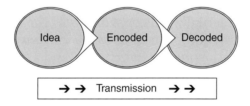

Figure 3.1 The communication process model

Idea: First, information exists in the mind of the sender; you cannot transmit it without first coding into some form that can be transmitted to the intended recipient(s). This can be a concept, idea, information, beliefs, values or emotion.

Encoding: Next, a message is transmitted to a recipient in an encoded form by the sender. This can take the form of spoken words, tone of voice, body language or written text.

Decoding: The recipient then decodes the words or symbols into simple information or as an idea that they can understand or reference to existing information.

COACHING SESSION 18

The communication process model

When considering the communication process model above, what do you think are the things that could impact on the flow or transmission of messages?

_____

_____

_____

_____

_____

_____

_____

_____

_____

When transmitting a message there are three things to keep in mind:

1. **Language:** This is the actual words or symbols of the message that was sent. This is not a reliable method by itself as words can have many meanings. Consider, for example, the phrases 'fat chance' and a 'slim chance', which both mean the same thing in English.

2. **Context:** This refers to the constraints of the circumstances that affect language use and variation. We have all heard the expression 'not to quote people out of context'. It is essential to take into account issues such as class, gender, race, space and age. Consider teenagers' 'text-speak' as an example.

3. **Paralanguage:** This is the way the message is delivered and can include the tone of voice, vocal intonation, body language, gestures and so forth. It can also include emotional responses such as anger, fear, happiness and so on. As humans, we frequently overestimate the accuracy of paralanguage. For example, most people believe that when someone is avoiding eye contact when talking this may suggest insincerity (even though this is not always the case).

A message has not been properly communicated unless it is understood by the recipient. To achieve good communication, we need to address the potential barriers to communication (Figure 3.2).

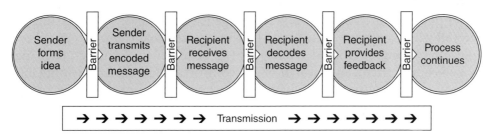

Figure 3.2 Barriers to communication model

We can see from this that barriers can appear at any (or all) of the stages in the transmission. We will examine these barriers to communication in some detail in the next chapter.

BODY LANGUAGE

Body language is the popular term for the process of communicating non-verbally through conscious or unconscious gestures and movements. This includes the subtle movements of the face and the body. In general usage, it can also include vocal tone, nuance and intonation. You may also see the terms 'kinesics' or 'paralanguage' being used, but most people today use the term 'body language'.

While you will often see claims that human communication consists of 93 per cent body language and that words account for only 7 per cent, this is false. It is based on a general misinterpretation of very specific research done by Albert Mehrabian in the 1960s in relation to the communication of feelings (Mehrabian & Ferris 1967). Very few writers seem to have bothered to read his actual research and continue to popularize the 93 per cent (or the 7%–38%–55%) fallacy.

Mehrabian himself states on his website:

> 'Please note ... equations regarding relative importance of verbal and nonverbal messages were derived from experiments dealing with communications of feelings and attitudes. Unless a communicator is talking about their feelings or attitudes, these equations are not applicable.'

> Mehrabian (2009)

This research cannot be extrapolated to communication in general. For example, can you watch a foreign film and still understand 93 per cent of what is happening? Does a book only convey 7 per cent of its meaning from the text? Obviously, this is just silly.

So just how important is body language? Well, it totally depends on the circumstances. Words are important and so are body gestures, vocal tone and eye movement. We discussed in Chapter 2 the limitations of email in conveying tone and we all know the limitations of telephone versus face-to-face communication.

The other popular myth about body language is that it is easy to read and that you can tell what someone is thinking by their gestures and movements. For example, a person with crossed arms is said to be 'defensive', though they may simply be keeping themselves warm or are comfortable in that position. Unless you know the person very well or have established a 'baseline' for their non-verbal communication, reading body language is extremely difficult. On the other hand, if you are talking to someone whose body language you have got to know well over time (e.g. a partner), then you may well be able to understand what it means when they 'touch their face'.

There are some key points to bear in mind when it comes to body language:

- Dismiss simplistic guides to complex issues such as non-verbal communication.

- Body language depends on the circumstances. What something 'means' in one situation may be very different in another.

- It is always better to look for clusters of gestures rather than trying to read a single gesture.

- Look for congruence: when a person's non-verbal and verbal communication do not match, there may be a problem.

- Proxemics is the word for the personal space aspect of body language. Personal space varies across cultures, and getting this right can be vital in an international setting.

 COACH'S TIP

Be aware of cultural differences in non-verbal communication

Certain gestures appear to be very similar in all people, for example smiling and fear. However, some body language is very specific to a particular group. Awareness of how your body language differs from others is a very valuable insight and a away to improve communication. In the next coaching session we will explore this issue in more detail.

COACHING SESSION 19

Body language

Have a look at the following non-verbal messages. What do they usually mean in your culture?

Non-verbal message	Typical interpretation
E.g. Making direct eye contact	E.g. secure, self-confident and assertive
Making direct eye contact	
Avoiding eye contact	
Nodding head	
Shaking head	
Scratching head	
Smiling	
Not smiling	
Folding or crossing arms	
Raising eyebrows	
Narrowing eyes	
Pointing a finger	
Thumbs up	
Biting lip	

Why not give this form to someone from a different culture and compare the answers with your own?

ONLINE RESOURCE

You can download a copy of this form by going to:

www.TYCoachbooks.com/Leadership

LISTENING SKILLS

'When people talk, listen completely. Most people never listen.'

Ernest Hemingway

At the heart of good communication is not the process of talking, but that of listening. The first step to improve your listening skills is to stop talking. It is very difficult to talk and listen at the same time.

A necessary component of listening is the proper use of silence. Most listeners speak as much as, if not more than, the person they are supposed to be listening to. Silence gives the other person:

- time to consider what they are going to say and to go deeper within themselves
- space to experience the feelings inside of them
- the opportunity to proceed at their own pace.

Great leaders need to develop their listening skills. Other practical tips to improve listening include the following:

- Don't interrupt.
- Paraphrase what you hear to make sure you have heard it correctly.
- Maintain appropriate eye contact.
- Lean towards the person.
- Use non-verbal cues to show that you are listening (nodding, saying 'Ah-ha' etc.).
- Be aware of 'body language'.
- Don't do anything else (e.g. surfing the web, checking your cell phone) while listening.
- Try to use both open and closed questions.
- Be empathetic – not sympathetic.
- Demonstrate acceptance.

COACH'S TIP

Communicate acceptance

When we are trying to communicate with another person we need to communicate acceptance. You do not want to communicate to the sender that it is not acceptable for them to feel the way they do. Try to avoid using phrases such as:

- 'You have to …' (*ordering*)
- 'You ought to …' (*moralizing*)
- 'Why don't you …' (*advising*)
- 'What you need … (*analysing*)
- 'You'll be fine …' (*sympathizing*)

Try to be an empathetic listener. Empathy is all about trying to understand the feelings of the sender – putting yourself in that person's shoes. True empathy is the ability to understand another's person's perspective. When you listen with empathy you set aside your own views and beliefs so that you can enter the other person's world.

'*…being empathic is a complex, demanding, strong yet subtle and gentle way of being.*'

Carl Rogers

COACHING SESSION 20

Listening quiz

So what are you like as a listener? Do you always listen with full attention or do you fall into the traps of poor listening? Take the following quiz to see what kind of listener you are.

Complete the following questionnaire as honestly as you can. Remember to answer questions according to how you really are and not how you hope to be.

STATEMENT	Never	Rarely	Sometimes	Often	Always
I finish other people's sentences before they have a chance to.	5	4	3	2	1
I paraphrase what I hear to make sure I have heard it correctly.	1	2	3	4	5
I show that I am engaged by maintaining eye contact, nodding and leaning forward.	1	2	3	4	5

STATEMENT	Never	Rarely	Sometimes	Often	Always
For me, listening is a passive process – I just sit there and try to listen.	5	4	③	2	1
For me, listening is an active process – I ask questions, make comments, etc.	1	2	③	4	5
I remind myself that listening is an opportunity to learn something.	1	2	3	④	5
Generally, I ignore 'body language', as you can learn more by just listening carefully.	5	④	3	2	1
I focus on the speaker's views and not on appearance.	1	2	3	④	5
I daydream while listening to someone express their thoughts or opinions.	5	④	3	2	1
I make myself listen even when the subject fails to interest me.	1	2	③	4	5
Normally, I've already made up my mind what certain types of people are going to say.	5	4	③	2	1
I say things like 'Ah-ha' or 'I understand', 'Go on' or nod, to let people know that I'm listening to them.	1	2	③	4	5
I often perform another task while listening to someone speak.	5	④	3	2	1
I try to use both open and closed questions in a discussion.	1	2	③	4	5
If someone mispronounces a word, I correct them.	5	4	③	2	1
Score					
Total score					

ONLINE RESOURCE

You can download the score interpretation as well as a copy of this quiz from:

www.TYCoachbooks.com/Leadership

Active listening

Active listening is a particular way of listening and responding to another person that improves mutual understanding. Often, when people talk to each other, they don't listen attentively. They are often distracted, half listening, half thinking about something else. They are usually busy formulating a response to what is being said. They assume that they have heard what the other person is saying many times before, so, rather than paying attention, they focus on how they can respond.

Active listening is a structured form of listening and responding that focuses the attention on the speaker. The listener must take care to attend to the speaker fully, and then repeat, in the listener's own words, what he or she thinks the speaker has said. The listener does not have to agree with the speaker – he or she must simply state what they think the speaker said. This allows the speaker to find out whether the listener really understood. If the listener did not, the speaker can explain some more.

Active listening has three fairly simple steps:

1. Encouraging responses
2. Reflecting the feelings of the speaker
3. Paraphrasing.

Encouraging responses

Here you simply encourage the person to continue talking without actually interrupting them. Nods of the head, simple fillers such as 'Ah-ha', 'Yes' and 'Go on' can work extremely well. You are letting the person know that you are listing to them and encouraging them to continue talking.

Reflecting the feelings of the speaker

Here you reflect (say back) to the person what you observe in them. For example, 'You seem really upset about that, John' or 'I can see that you seem really worried, Jane' can let the person know that you are actively listening to them. If you get the reflection wrong, they will normally simply correct you with a statement like 'No, I'm not angry, just really sad.' Reflecting feeling is required when using active listening.

Paraphrasing

This is probably the most important of the three steps. Here you carefully listen to what the person is saying and then repeat, in your own words, what you think the speaker has said. You don't have to agree with the other person – simply state what you think they said. For example: 'So what you are telling me, Ahmed, is that you are really behind on your work and you think it's because of the new software?' If Ahmed believes you have it right, he will respond with a non-verbal nod or with a 'Yes, that's exactly it.' Ahmed will feel listened to. If you have heard him incorrectly, he will correct you.

Active listening has real benefits. First, it forces people to listen attentively to others. Second, it avoids misunderstandings, as people have to confirm that they do really understand what another person has said. Third, it tends to open people up, to get them to say more. You cannot use active listening all the time. Choose those situations when you need to clearly understand what someone has to say. Good examples would be in interviews, when giving feedback and in any conversation with a difficult emotional content.

NEXT STEPS

In this chapter we have seen that, for communication to be successful, it is essential that the receiver gives the same meaning to the message as intended by the sender of the message. We saw some of the myths about body language and also the actual facts. We have looked at the importance of listening and the use of active listening.

In the next chapter we will look at look at the barriers to communication and the possible solutions to them. Removing barriers to communication is one of the easiest ways to improve communication. Removing these barriers is not always easy, but it's worth the effort.

TAKEAWAYS

What is communication?

_____

_____

_____

_____

_____

_____

_____

_____

_____

_____

_____

_____

_____

What is effective and what is ineffective communication?

_____

_____

_____

_____

_____

_____

_____

_____

_____

_____

_____

_____

_____

What is active listening and when should you use it?

_____

_____

_____

_____

_____

_____

_____

_____

_____

BARRIERS TO COMMUNICATION

4

✔ OUTCOMES FROM THIS CHAPTER

- Know that communication is not always perfect – problems can easily arise.
- Understand that there are many barriers to communication.

'What we've got here is failure to communicate!'

The Captain in *Cool Hand Luke* (1967)

To achieve good communication, we need to address the potential barriers to communication. We saw in the previous chapter that for communication to be successful, it is necessary that the receiver applies the same meaning to the message as was planned by the sender. But, as we know, communication is not always perfect. At times, some meaning is lost as the message encounters various barriers as it is transmitted from the sender to the receiver.

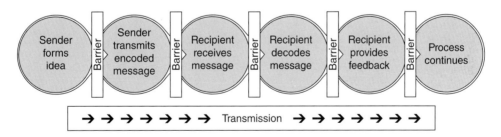

Figure 4.1 Barriers to communication model

We can see in Figure 4.1 that barriers can appear at any (or all) of the stages in the transmission:

- when the sender forms an idea (stereotyping, generational, language, etc.)
- when an idea is encoded (jargon, overload, perception, etc.)

- when the recipient receives the message (noise, stress, distractions, etc.)
- when the recipient decodes the message (history, stress, overload, etc.)
- when the recipient gives feedback verbally or non-verbally (emotion, retention, culture).

Then the process or cycle of communication continues.

COACHING SESSION 21

Barriers to communication

Try to come up with a list of seven barriers to communication based on your own experiences as a leader and in your life.

1 _____

_____

2 _____

_____

3 _____

_____

4 _____

_____

5 _____

_____

6 _____

_____

7 _____

From this list select the **three** most serious for you and expand on them below:

Barrier	Why is this a problem for you?
1	
2	
3	

As we have seen, barriers may occur at any of the stages through which a message passes during the process. These barriers include the following:

- **Physical:** These are obvious and include closed doors, office partitioning and distance between people.

- **You:** Focusing on yourself rather than the other person leads to lack of empathy. Empathy is not the same as sympathy, which tends to produce rather than minimize barriers.

- **Perception:** This is about how we understand the world around us. Everyone has their own perceptions of the world, formed by experience, knowledge and attitudes over time. Because of this difference in perceptions, different individuals respond to the same message in different ways. For example, if you send your message believing that the person you are talking to will not understand what you have to say, you may end up unconsciously sabotaging your effort to communicate.

- **Interpersonal:** Some people find it more difficult than others to form genuine connections with others. Others see themselves as 'social beings'. Interpersonal communication skills are something we have been developing since early childhood. For example, if you come from a family where children were taught to 'be seen and not heard', and were punished for expressing an opinion, you may have developed into an adult who lacks confidence.

- **Overload:** Leaders are constantly bombarded with a barrage of information. It is necessary to manage this information flow, or we will not receive the relevant information. For all the benefits of the so-called 'communications revolution', information overload rather than the 'paperless office' has been the result. This leads to problems such as messages not returned, rushed discussions and poor decision making.

- **Emotion:** Emotional barriers can be difficult to overcome, but are important to be aware of and manage. The emotional state of a person affects their communication. For example, if the receiver believes that the sender is angry, the receiver may put up barriers before the sender even has a chance to speak.

- **Language:** Language barriers can be the difficulties faced when people, who have no language in common, try to communicate. But it can also refer to people talking too fast, too softly or using too much jargon. Certain words also can be 'triggers' for negative reactions and hinder good communication. For example, if someone uses the word 'chairman' instead of 'chairperson', you may focus on the word and not the message.

- **Jargon:** This is the use of over-complicated, unfamiliar and/or technical terms. Consider the term 'pushing the envelope'. This basically means to go outside what is seen as normal corporate boundaries in order to attain a goal. But you can imagine the confusion this term might cause someone who has never heard it before!

- **Physiology:** Physiological barriers are associated with the limitations of the human body and the human mind (e.g. memory). However, problems can also arise out of other physiological problems such as speech dyspraxia/ verbal dyspraxia (a motor co-ordination difficulty affecting pronunciation); phonological difficulty (using the wrong sounds in speech) or even dementia, where difficulties with speech are often the first noticeable symptoms.

- **Gender:** Gender barriers have become less of an issue in recent years, but there is still the possibility for gender confusion in communication. One researcher, Susan Herring, conducted a study on email communications and found an apparent difference in the language used online. She found that men are more prone to write in an aggressive, competitive style, while women tend to be far more supportive in their writing (Herring 1994).

■ **Generational:** Whether you are a baby boomer (born between 1949 and 1965), a Generation X (born between 1965 and 1980) or a Generation Y or Millennial (born between 1981 and 1999), your ways of communicating are shaped by the generation you were brought up in. On a recent training course a delegate in their 50s complained loudly that the younger members rarely returned phone calls by phone. Instead, they typically would text or email a response. What she was failing to see was the difference in generational communication styles.

■ **Culture:** Culture shapes the way we think and behave. The norms of communication vary greatly in different cultures, as does the way in which people communicate. For example, silence is greatly respected and widely used in Japan, whereas in the UK people are likely to fill the gaps in communications with more words. (See Chapter 10.)

■ **Taboos:** Some people may find it difficult to express their emotions and some topics may be completely 'off-limits' or taboo. In their book *Forbidden Words: Taboo and the Censoring of Language*, Keith Allan and Kate Burridge suggest that, in contemporary Western society, taboo and euphemism are closely entwined with ideas of politeness and 'face' (basically, a person's self-image). People have to consider whether what they are saying will maintain, enhance, or damage their own face, as well as to be considerate of the face needs of others (Allan & Burridge 2006).

■ **Stereotyping:** Stereotyping allows us to simplify our complex world because it reduces the amount of thinking we have to do when we meet a new person. However, we usually see negative rather than positive images when stereotyping and it should generally be avoided. If you group races or individuals together and make a judgement or generalization about them, your perception is likely to be inaccurate.

■ **Distractions:** If communication is to succeed, we must, as far as is possible, remove distractions. Distractions come in many forms, both in the office and at home. They include cell phones, tablets, email programs, desk distractions (paperwork, gadgets and photos), television, noise and music. This is not an exhaustive list but they all have the same effect – a lack of attention resulting in communication breakdown.

■ **Time:** Communicating effectively takes time. If you fail to dedicate the time necessary, you will encounter problems. For example, if you feel rushed you are unlikely to be paying full attention to the other person, allowing silences for thinking or concentrating on the sent messages.

■ **Stress:** When we are feeling stressed, the physical and emotional impact can severely impair good communication. When we are stressed, good listening and clear reflection are severely limited.

- **History:** Previous experiences with a person or particular situation may make us biased towards how we believe they are going to respond to what we communicate. For example, a junior employee who is always facing negative feedback from those in authority will ultimately limit their communication with you to a management interview.

- **Retention:** Human memory cannot function beyond particular physiological and psychological constraints. We do not always retain what is being said, particularly if we are not interested in what is being said. For example, can you remember the last talk you had with that boring person at a social function?

- **Noise:** Equipment or other environmental noises can hinder communication. The sender and the receiver must both be able to hear and concentrate on the messages being sent.

COACHING SESSION 22

Barrier list

Compare the list of 20 barriers above with your seven barriers from Coaching session 21. Were your seven all included? List any additional ones here:

_____

_____

_____

_____

_____

_____

_____

_____

_____

_____

_____

_____

_____

_____

COACHING SESSION 23

Personal experiences of barriers

Complete this next coaching session by coming up with an example from your own experiences for each of the 20 barriers given above.

Barrier	Your example
Physical	
You	
Perception	
Interpersonal	
Overload	
Emotion	
Language	
Jargon	
Physiology	

Barrier	Your example
Gender	
Generational	
Culture	
Taboos	
Stereotyping	
Distractions	
Time	
Stress	
History	
Retention	
Noise	

IMPROVING YOUR COMMUNICATION SKILLS

When we looked at the barriers to communication, you probably were already thinking about the possible solutions for each of these. Let's now look at each of the 20 in turn and the possible solutions to each of them. Removing barriers to communication is one of the easiest ways to improve communication. Removing these barriers is not always easy, but it's always worthwhile.

COACHING SESSION 24

Barriers to communication: solutions

For each of the 20 barriers, try to answer the question set below by yourself. Following each question you can see what the experts recommend about removing or reducing each barrier. For each, see how close your answer is to what is proposed. If you get stuck on a particular barrier, feel free to read ahead to get a tip!

Physical

How would you go about removing or limiting the communication problems caused by 'physical' barriers?

_____

_____

_____

_____

_____

_____

_____

_____

Possible solution: While the problems here may be obvious, the solutions are not always so obvious. Of course, you can open closed doors, limit office partitioning, and so on, but sometimes more is needed. While email and telephone are valuable tools, don't let them dominate your communication strategy. Speak to people; take time to visit someone's space. Great leaders make use of interpersonal communication and always try to remove as many physical barriers to communication as is possible. If you are going to have an 'open door policy', first don't use that term – it annoys people! Secondly, make sure that you really do have an open door. Do your people know what it means? What are the limits? – and there will be limits. Make sure these are communicated.

You

How would you go about removing or limiting the communication problems caused by 'you' barriers?

_____

_____

_____

_____

_____

_____

_____

Possible solution: Focus on the other person, not on yourself. Pay close attention to what is being said (and *not* said). Show people that you are paying attention by squarely facing the person; maintain an open posture, lean slightly towards them and use appropriate eye contact. The key here, as elsewhere, is to demonstrate good listening skills. Don't have sympathy, show empathy, and make sure that you understand the difference.

Perception

How would you go about removing or limiting the communication problems caused by 'perception' barriers?

_____

_____

_____

_____

_____

_____

_____

Possible solution: Be aware of your own biases and assumptions. Accept that different individuals respond to the same message in their own unique way. Try to limit your assumptions and approach each opportunity as a chance to learn. Try to use 'I' messages rather than 'you' messages. 'I' messages were originally studied by Dr Haim Ginott, a noted child psychologist, who suggested that statements beginning with 'I' are less provocative than those starting with 'you'. An example of this would be to say, 'I really am getting behind in my work because I don't have the financial report yet,' rather than 'You didn't complete the financial report on time!'

Interpersonal

How would you go about removing or limiting the communication problems caused by 'interpersonal' barriers?

_____

_____

_____

_____

_____

_____

_____

_____

Possible solution: Have a positive attitude to communication. Try to approach communication as an important leadership activity rather than something to 'get out of the way'. Experiment with communication techniques. What works with one person may not work well with another. Vary methods, listening techniques and feedback methods. If you find it hard to form genuine connections with others, ask yourself why. Consider this as a task to master and possibly seek help from a mentor or coach.

Overload

How would you go about removing or limiting the communication problems caused by 'overload' barriers?

_____

_____

_____

_____

_____

_____

_____

_____

Possible solution: Addressing overload requires self-discipline. Find time to focus, filter out the daily 'spam' and focus on what is essential. For example, checking your email two or three times a day – rather than continually – may enable you to better focus on effective email communications. Don't multitask; focus on one thing at a time. Current research indicates that multitasking unequivocally damages productivity. (See Chapter 2.)

Emotion

How would you go about removing or limiting the communication problems caused by 'emotion' barriers?

_____

_____

_____

_____

_____

_____

_____

Possible solution: Do not ignore the emotional context in communication. Keep an open mind, and learn about your own biases that may interfere with the transfer of information. Try reflecting back to the person what you perceive to be their emotional state. Research from the world of counselling has shown that communication is enhanced when you reflect feelings – for example, 'It sounds like you're feeling really angry about this change' or 'You seem pretty irritated by that customer's feedback.' When you reflect feelings in this way, the person can correct you if you are reading things wrongly, and where you are correct they will feel understood.

Language

How would you go about removing or limiting the communication problems caused by 'language' barriers?

_____

_____

_____

_____

_____

_____

_____

Possible solution: When we don't share the same words as another person, non-verbal communication becomes even more necessary. Remember: language is not just about nationality, it is also about regional accent, technical language and even the language of leadership. One interesting research finding is that when we use a similar language to another person we can establish rapport. This is a method often used by experienced salespeople. It seems that people like people who are like themselves.

Jargon

How would you go about removing or limiting the communication problems caused by 'jargon' barriers?

_____

_____

_____

_____

_____

_____

_____

Possible solution: To be blunt: stop using overcomplicated, unfamiliar and/or technical terms. Unless you are sure that the person you are communicating with understands the term, don't use it. Don't use 'big words' to impress (they don't), to seem important (you won't), or to impress your team (it won't). Try to avoid leadership clichés such as: 'thinking outside the box', 'giving it 110 per cent' and 'paradigm shift'. Also, when talking to someone who speaks a different language from you, avoid acronyms. In fact, I have an acronym for that – AAA (Avoid Annoying Acronyms).

Physiology

How would you go about removing or limiting the communication problems caused by 'physiology' barriers?

_____

_____

_____

_____

_____

_____

_____

_____

Possible solution: Sometimes it can be difficult to understand how to communicate with people who may have physical or mental-health issues. Communication problems might result from a physical condition such as hearing difficulties or visual impairment, or as a result of a condition affecting the brain, such as Alzheimer's or a stroke. These communication problems may be evident in people you lead or in people you work with (NHS 2013).

Be aware of issues such as your tone of voice, how fast you speak and how you use body language. You also need to be aware of how your own reactions may affect other people's ability to communicate.

Gender

How would you go about removing or limiting the communication problems caused by 'gender' barriers?

_____

_____

_____

_____

_____

_____

_____

Possible solution: John Gray's bestselling book *Men Are from Mars, Women Are from Venus* highlights the differences in how men and women think, with a focus on personal relationships. However, such differences are over-exaggerated as women's and men's communication styles are in practice very close. For example, both women and men can be nurturing, aggressive or passive. What is important is that women and men sometimes perceive the same messages to have different meanings. Studies show that women, to a greater degree than men, are sensitive to the interpersonal meanings that lie 'between the lines' in the messages they exchange. Men, on the other hand – to a greater extent than women – are more sensitive to 'between the lines meanings' about status (Wood 2009).

Generational

How would you go about removing or limiting the communication problems caused by 'generational' barriers?

_____

_____

_____

_____

_____

_____

_____

_____

_____

Possible solution: The great American author and humourist Mark Twain is believed to have said: 'When I was a boy of fourteen, my father was so ignorant I could hardly stand to have the old man around. But when I got to be twenty-one, I was astonished by how much he'd learned in seven years.' Intergenerational communication can be challenging. However, in many ways this is a similar answer to the gender issue above. Generational differences are often over-exaggerated. People of all ages can be open, aggressive or intuitive. What is important is that people can perceive the same messages to have different meanings. The key is to understand the differences and appreciate that people of different generations sometimes communicate using different filters.

Culture

How would you go about removing or limiting the communication problems caused by 'cultural' barriers?

_____

_____

_____

_____

_____

_____

_____

Possible solution: When we communicate across cultures it is important to recognize the complexity and differences that exist. We should try to listen more actively and ask questions. We need to be flexible, honest and avoid stereotyping (see below). If we respect differences and sometimes just 'think twice' before speaking, we can minimize potential problems. The golden rule is, if in doubt, ask. I've never met anyone who is not happy to explain what a gesture, behaviour, word or expression means from their own cultural background. (See Chapter 10.)

Taboos

How would you go about removing or limiting the communication problems caused by 'taboo' barriers?

_____

_____

_____

_____

_____

_____

_____

Possible solution: Taboos are often rooted in the beliefs of the people of a specific culture and are handed down from generation to generation. Understanding communication taboos and what to avoid is an important skill for any manager. You need to learn about these taboos to be an effective leader.

Accept that some people may find it difficult to communicate about particular topics and some may be completely off-limits. Always consider whether what you are saying will maintain, enhance or damage your 'face', and also be considerate of the 'face' needs of others. Ask yourself whether discussion of the topic is necessary or whether it will enhance your relationship with the other person. Respecting other people's taboos is a sign of emotional intelligence (see Chapter 11).

Stereotyping

How would you go about removing or limiting the communication problems caused by 'stereotyping' barriers?

_____

_____

_____

_____

_____

_____

_____

Possible solution: Stereotyping is useful as it allows us to simplify our complex world, yet most people usually see negative rather than positive images when stereotyping. Stereotyping results in us ignoring differences between individuals and we therefore make generalizations. These generalizations create barriers to effective communication.

Think of a time when you were guilty of stereotyping. Ask yourself how correct your assumptions were when you got to know the person. Chances are that your assumptions were wrong. Try to apply critical thinking and the application of facts in place of stereotyping.

Distractions

How would you go about removing or limiting the communication problems caused by 'distractions' barriers?

_____

_____

_____

_____

_____

_____

_____

_____

Possible solution: If you want to communicate without barriers, you need to actively remove distractions. While it is not always possible to remove all distractions in any given circumstance, you need to try to minimize them as much as possible. Never try to communicate with someone while doing something else. For example, can you remember when you were talking to someone over the telephone and you just knew they were working on their computer, even though you couldn't see it.

Distractions come in many forms; smartphones and tablets are a significant one in today's society. Never try to communicate with another person while focusing on your screen. But also consider *where* you try to communicate, and adjust your environment to improve communication flow. Closing blinds to block out the view, turning off a monitor or removing clutter from your desk can be a great way of saying 'I'm interested in what you are saying.'

Time

How would you go about removing or limiting the communication problems caused by 'time' barriers?

_____

_____

_____

_____

_____

_____

_____

Possible solution: Attempting to communicate in a rushed way is potentially disastrous. For example, if you feel rushed, you are unlikely to be paying full attention to the other person. Effective communication without barriers needs time. If you don't have enough time – don't start the conversation. Wait until you do.

As a leader, always plan enough time in your diary for communication with staff and clients. Communicating effectively takes time and you need to allow for the differences between different people. Be particularly aware of potential cultural and generational differences.

Stress

How would you go about removing or limiting the communication problems caused by 'stress' barriers?

_____

_____

_____

_____

_____

_____

_____

Possible solution: When you are feeling stressed, effective communication is severely limited. Unless you have to have that meeting or interview, try to reschedule for a time when you are more relaxed. Trying to fit someone in for a 'quick talk' when you are 'stressed out' is not a good idea.

If you must proceed, take a few minutes to try to relax. Take a few deep breaths or get a couple of minutes of fresh air; even a few minutes of meditation can calm you enough to continue.

History

How would you go about removing or limiting the communication problems caused by 'history' barriers?

_____

_____

_____

_____

_____

_____

_____

_____

_____

Possible solution: Previous experiences with a person or a particular situation may make us biased about how we believe they are going to respond to what we communicate. Be aware of these personal 'triggers' and try to avoid preconceptions. An open mind is essential for effective communication.

If you have 'history' with a particular person, be aware of the impact that this is having on you when you communicate with them. If a particular situation has always gone a particular way, tell yourself that it doesn't always have to go that way. People and things can change. Be open to that change or you may find yourself repeating negative patterns of communication indefinitely.

Retention

How would you go about removing or limiting the communication problems caused by 'retention' barriers?

_____

_____

_____

_____

_____

_____

_____

Possible solution: Be aware that your memory cannot function beyond certain physiological and psychological constraints. We do not always retain what is being said, particularly if we are not interested in what is being said or are distracted. Active listening can help (see Chapter 3) but sometimes we may need to resort to other memory tools. Taking notes, for example, is not always conducive to open communication, but it is better to take notes (possibly apologizing for doing so) than not to retain important parts of a discussion.

Sometimes using techniques such as mind-mapping or writing up diary notes after an important discussion can be very helpful. The key point here is to be aware of your own limitations and constraints and their likely impact on communication.

Noise

How would you go about removing or limiting the communication problems caused by 'noise' barriers?

_____

_____

_____

_____

_____

_____

_____

Possible solution: Noise can be a barrier to effective communication. Be aware of your environment and evaluate the level of equipment or other noises in your space. If the sender and the receiver can't hear each other properly, they will not be able to concentrate on the messages being sent. As with the distractions above, consider how to minimize these if you want to promote clear communication. It is better to move a meeting to another location than to persevere when noise means people can't hear what is being said. If a phone line is noisy, redial or change devices. Take time to prepare your environment so that noise is limited and communication is enhanced.

→ NEXT STEPS

In this chapter we have looked at the barriers to communication and the possible solutions to them. Removing barriers to communication is one of the easiest ways to improve communication. Removing these barriers is not always easy, but it repays the effort richly.

In the next chapter we will look at teams and teamwork. We will look at the difference between a group and a team and how teams are formed. We will ask what characterizes high-performing teams and how we should build and maintain them.

TAKEAWAYS

What is a communication barrier?

_____

_____

_____

_____

_____

_____

_____

_____

_____

_____

_____

What are the main barriers to effective communication that have occurred in your own experience?

_____

_____

_____

_____

_____

_____

_____

_____

_____

_____

_____

What can you do about removing these barriers?

_____

_____

_____

_____

_____

_____

_____

_____

_____

_____

TEAMS AND TEAMWORK 5

 OUTCOMES FROM THIS CHAPTER

- Understand how teams are formed.
- Know what makes a team effective.
- Learn how to build an effective team.
- Discover how team building helps a team develop competencies.

'Michael, if you can't pass, you can't play.'

Coach Dean Smith to Michael Jordan in his freshman year at UNC

Individuals do not usually work in isolation. Work is essentially a group-based activity and, if an organization is to be effective, it requires effective teamworking at all levels. Indeed, teamworking has become an increasingly common feature of organizational life as management seeks to introduce flatter organizational structures in response to changes in technology in an increasingly complex marketplace.

When working effectively, a team can provide real benefits for both individuals and organizations, but you should also be aware of the pitfalls of teamworking. If you simply call a group of people who work together a team, you will not magically harness the real benefits of teamworking. This chapter examines the key ingredients of successful team performance, which will help you build and develop teams within your organization.

COACHING SESSION 25

Definition of a team

How would you define a team? Try to write this in 25 words or fewer.

_____

_____

_____

_____

_____

_____

_____

It is important to be clear on our definition of a team. There has been a preoccupation by work psychologists with debating the differences between teams and groups. Simply said, a team is a particular type of group. A team can be defined as two or more people, who come together in a group to achieve a common goal or objective which is not achievable on an individual basis.

Teamworking as a method of organizing people at work has potential benefits at an individual level – in terms of satisfying various psychological needs – and at an organizational level – in terms of performing functions to achieve organizational objectives.

Examples of teams within organizations can include:

- **management teams** whose members are brought together to determine strategic objectives

- **project teams** whose members are brought together for a limited time from different functions within the organization to achieve a particular purpose

- **production teams** whose members are responsible for performing day-to-day core operations.

COACHING SESSION 26

Types of team

What kinds of team are you a member of? List them below.

_____

_____

_____

_____

_____

_____

_____

_____

_____

_____

In recent years, particularly within manufacturing, there has been a move towards self-managed teams where the team takes on responsibilities usually assigned to managers, such as planning, organizing, directing and staffing. The most famous example of this kind of work organization occurred during the 1970s at Volvo's Kalmar plant in Sweden. The company moved away from the traditional assembly line to self-managed teams where groups of employees were given responsibility for building a complete car from start to finish, checking quality, problem solving and achieving production targets.

STAGES OF TEAM DEVELOPMENT

Dr Bruce Tuckman's 'Forming, Storming, Norming, Performing and Adjourning' model (Figure 5.1) is probably the best known among the various theories about how teams are made. With its clever phrasing and simple concepts, it is often used by facilitators to help groups understand how they can become more effective. Tuckman first published it in 1965 and he added the fifth stage, 'Adjourning', after a review of the theory in the mid-1970s (Tuckman & Jensen 1977).

Figure 5.1 Tuckman team formation model (Tuckman 1965)

To come up with the theory, Tuckman reviewed academic research and theory papers. From these, he identified that all groups initially appear to have sequential development stages in common. These are:

- **Forming:** This is the 'getting to know you' stage, where individual members share information about themselves and about the purpose of the group. This stage is typically associated with polite conversation and with underlying tension and anxieties as members try to clarify their objectives.

- **Storming:** This is perhaps the most critical stage of group development. It is associated with a release of tension and anxiety as individual members begin to disagree and challenge one another's views. Power struggles may emerge here. Members may begin to question the purpose of the group, challenge earlier decisions, become impatient about the lack of progress and resent the roles allocated to them. You should note that conflict is a healthy process. It can be managed to bring the group together. (See Chapter 8.)

- **Norming:** This stage involves the group establishing clearly defined ways of working together. Shared expectations of behaviour acceptable to group members are communicated and agreed, which can include the allocation of roles to achieve the group's objectives, attendance, participation, agendas and basic conversational courtesies. In other words, the group agrees on the ground rules for what will and will not be tolerated in the group.

- **Performing:** At this stage, the group has settled its relationships and expectations. All the interpersonal issues have been resolved so the group is now at the stage of getting on with achieving its objectives. This last stage is characterized by a high degree of cohesiveness and commitment to the group. This is where we want a team to be.

- **Adjourning:** At this point, the group task comes to an end and people return to their roles as individuals. There may be a degree of sadness among group members, so some people call this the 'mourning' stage. It can be important to have ceremonies or other methods of 'closure' to support the team at this stage.

It is, of course, not possible to specify how long it will take a team to work through these different stages of development and you may find that some teams skip stages. Some teams may take months to work through the various stages while others pass through them very quickly because of time pressures. Teams whose members already know one another and have established effective ways of working together may move directly to the latter stages.

Some work psychologists wonder whether team development can really be described in such a linear way. Teams and individuals tend to deviate from developing in predictable ways, so there are bound to be overlaps between stages and a level of ambiguity about what happens when. However, Tuckman's model remains a useful one for helping us understand something as complex as a team.

COACHING SESSION 27

Team stages

Consider a team you have joined in the recent past. Try to describe in the boxes below what happened at each of the stages. Did the group become 'stuck' at any stage? What was done about this? Be as descriptive as you can when you write about each stage.

Forming

Storming

Norming

Performing

Adjourning

EFFECTIVE AND INEFFECTIVE TEAMS

What makes a team effective? Obviously, it can be when it gets the job done that it was set up to do. But things are always more complex than that. Do you believe that there are common 'building blocks' that make up an effective team? What about an ineffective team – what qualities does it lack?

COACHING SESSION 28

Effective and ineffective teams

Try listing the qualities or 'building blocks' you think make up an effective team and the factors that lead to an ineffective team. Think about your own experiences here with teams you have been part of in the past.

Effective	Ineffective
Example: Clear objectives	*Example:* Poor communication

BUILDING AN EFFECTIVE TEAM

Work psychologists have devised numerous frameworks to help managers discover what makes an effective team. Probably the one which is most widely known and applied within organizations is the work of Meredith R. Belbin, which was first publicized in his bestselling book *Management Teams: Why They Succeed or Fail* in 1981. Over a period of nine years, Belbin invited practising managers to take part in a business simulation game, which was run over a weekend. When Belbin analysed the behaviours of successful teams, he found that these managers were able to perform a wide range of roles, due to their varied mix of personalities and abilities.

Although Belbin clearly defined nine team roles, he did not mean that a successful team should have nine members. His research showed that a team member could take on more than one team role, and frequently two or three. However, he cautioned against members taking on a role which did not suit their abilities or personality. Belbin's research is useful as it shows how we all have our strengths and weaknesses as team members. In a successful team, our weaknesses are balanced out by the strengths of others.

Once you have your team roles balanced and you have effective communication strategies in place, the next step is to improve team competencies. These competencies are not just those held by individual team members but are competencies that are developed and shared by members of the team. Team building refers to a wide variety of activities, designed to improve team performance.

Team building is an ongoing process that helps a team develop relevant competencies. The team members not only share expectations for accomplishing group tasks, but trust and support one another and respect one another's individual differences. Your role as a leader is to lead your team towards cohesiveness and productivity.

TEAM COMPETENCIES – HIGH-PERFORMING TEAMS

There are several theories about which competencies are possessed by high-performing teams. But most theorists agree that the following seven competencies are the most important.:

1. The team focuses on open and effective communication techniques.

2. The team has clear, measurable goals that are accepted by all members.

3. The team has proven decision-making strategies, team members influence decisions, and there is an emphasis on consensus-based methods.

4. The team holds its members mutually accountable for results.

5. The team has a process for managing conflicts but also appreciates the positive aspects of conflict (e.g. it avoids 'groupthink').

6. Team members collaborate with one another to accomplish their goals.

7. Team members are willing to take risks to bring new, innovative ideas that will assist the team to achieve desired results.

COACHING SESSION 29

Assessment of team competencies

Think of a team you are presently leading or are a part of. Use the following assessment tool to evaluate team competencies based on the seven points above.

Please respond according to how the team is (rather than how you think you think it should be), and don't worry if some statements seem to score in the 'wrong direction'. When you are finished, total up your score and read the interpretation box to see what it means.

Team name or description:	Date:				
STATEMENT	Never	Rarely	Sometimes	Often	Always
Team members communicate in an open and productive way with each other.	1	2	3	4	5
In this team people listen to each other.	1	2	3	4	5
The team sets clear and measurable goals.	1	2	3	4	5
We are never quite sure where we are going as a team.	5	4	3	2	1
The team knows how to effectively make decisions.	1	2	3	4	5
The team uses various 'tools' to make decisions (brainstorming, force-field analysis, etc.).	1	2	3	4	5
When something goes wrong, team members usually blame one other.	5	4	3	2	1
We see success as a 'team' rather than an 'individual' thing.	1	2	3	4	5
Conflict is avoided at all costs.	5	4	3	2	1
The team manages conflict effectively.	1	2	3	4	5
Competition rather than collaboration is the norm.	5	4	3	2	1
Team members work well together on projects.	1	2	3	4	5
As a team, we avoid risk.	5	4	3	2	1
We usually stop and critique how well we are working together.	1	2	3	4	5
Others describe the team as an effective one.	1	2	3	4	5
Score					
Total score					

Score interpretation

Score	Comment
15–30	Your team has problems. It is not functioning well. The team is at an immature or low competency level, and team building is needed. Review the seven competencies above and try to pinpoint where things are going wrong. Have a look again at the Tuckman stages – have you got stuck somewhere? What about the Belbin roles – is there a team deficit? Remember that communication is the single most significant factor in successful teamwork – this would appear to be a problem with this team.
31–50	This would indicate that your team is doing OK but could do better. A score in this range indicates that competency is at a mid-level, and there is still work to be done by the team and team leader. Consider talking to the team about this result. With a bit more effort you can move to the high-performing category. Are there some areas where you drop points? If so, work on them as a team.
50–75	This is a high-performing team. Well done! Don't be complacent; good teamwork is an ongoing endeavour. Keep striving for excellence and don't stop communicating. Is this team effectiveness rewarded and acknowledged? Given how well your team is doing, consider how you would feed back this information to the team.

Given your result, what do you need to do to further develop your team? Consider the seven competencies above – is your team weak in one over others? Why not get everyone in your team to complete the assessment and compare results?

_____

_____

_____

_____

_____

_____

_____

_____

ONLINE RESOURCE

You can download this team assessment form by going to:

www.TYCoachbooks.com/Leadership

NEXT STEPS

In this chapter we have looked at teams and team building. We saw that team building is an ongoing process that helps a team develop relevant competencies. There are many theories about which competencies are possessed by high-performing teams, but we looked at seven key competencies that really make a difference.

In the next chapter we will look at strategy and strategic thinking. 'Strategy' and 'strategic thinking' have many possible definitions and can be very confusing. We will try to simplify the fundamental ideas about strategy and strategic thinking that are necessary for you to acquire as a leader.

TAKEAWAYS

What is a team?

_____

_____

_____

_____

_____

_____

_____

_____

_____

_____

What is the theory put forward by Tuckman and what can we learn from it about how teams develop?

_____

_____

_____

_____

_____

_____

_____

_____

_____

_____

_____

_____

Can you list the seven key competencies possessed by high-performing teams?

_____

_____

_____

_____

_____

_____

_____

_____

_____

_____

_____

STRATEGY AND STRATEGIC THINKING

✔ OUTCOMES FROM THIS CHAPTER

- Understand the difficulties of trying to define strategy.
- Learn how strategy can be applied to different levels of an organization.
- Realize the importance of having a clear strategy.
- Acquire the tools you can use to think about strategy.

'You may not be interested in strategy, but strategy is interested in you.'

Leon Trotsky

So just what is strategy? A simple dictionary-type definition would be something like: 'A plan of action designed to achieve a major or overall aim.' The word itself comes from the Greek στρατηγία – *stratēgia* – which basically means 'generalship' or 'office of general'. In the world of business, it is often seen as attaining and maintaining a competitive advantage.

🗣 COACHING SESSION 30

Defining strategy

How do you define strategy? Have a go now.

_____

_____

_____

_____

_____

_____

There is not much consensus about strategy from the experts. *The Economist* (1993: 106) observed: 'The consultants and theorists jostling to advise businesses cannot even agree on the most basic of all questions: what, precisely, is a Corporate Strategy.' One writer, Markides (1999), admits: 'We simply do not know what strategy is or how to develop a good one.' 'Strategy' clearly has many possible definitions, and this in itself can be very confusing. At the most simple level, strategy is how you get from where you are now to where you want to be. It is worth thinking of this as a three-step process, as shown in Figure 6.1.

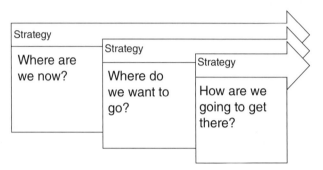

Figure 6.1 The strategy process

This seems pretty simple, but the process is more difficult than it seems at first. First of all, you need to have a very clear idea of where you actually are. This involves knowing your strengths and weaknesses. It means understanding your competition and your place in the market. How do customers see your business, and what threats do you face as an organization?

Then you need to know where it is you want to be. This requires you to look ahead to the future. This is about your future environment, future options, future competitive advantages and your future goals.

And finally you need to know how you are going to get to where you want to go. This is possibly the most important and often most overlooked stage. Any strategy needs to be described in clear, specific terms if it is to have any chance of succeeding.

COACHING SESSION 31

Strategy and your organization

Does your organization have a 'corporate strategy'? Is it written down anywhere (website, intranet, corporate documents)? See if you can find it now and copy it out below. Does it include the three areas in the diagram above?

Corporate strategy (write out a brief summary)	
Does it cover... (If yes – explain how; if no – explain why not.)	
...where we are now	Yes ☐ No ☐
...where we want to go	Yes ☐ No ☐
...how we are going to get there	Yes ☐ No ☐

LEVEL OF STRATEGY

Strategy can be applied to different levels of an organization. Generally, it can be categorized into four areas. These are:

1. **Organizational level strategy:** This is concerned with the overall design and scope of the business. This is usually focused on stakeholders (owners, shareholders, government, etc.). Corporate strategy is often stated explicitly in 'mission' and 'vision' statements. This level of strategy is supposed to guide strategic decision-making throughout the organization.

2. **Functional level strategy:** The focus here is on business units such as production, marketing, sales, etc. The focus is usually on competition and strategic decisions about how to achieve the corporate strategy.

3. **Human resource (HR) strategy:** The focus here, depending on the HR philosophy of the organization, is how to develop the skills, attitudes and behaviours of staff and others so that the organization meets its strategic goals.

4. **Team strategy:** Depending on how teams are viewed in the organization, this is concerned with how teams are organized to deliver the organizational, functional and HR strategic directions.

COACHING SESSION 32

Level of strategy

Thinking about an organization you know well, can you describe examples of strategy for each of these levels? Be as descriptive as you can.

Level	Example
Organizational	
Functional	
Human resource (HR)	
Team	

COACHING SESSION 33

Clarity of your strategy

Take one level of strategy from above (probably the one you are most familiar with) and score it in terms of the clarity with which you understand its essential ingredients in the assessment tool below.

Strategy characteristics	Very clear	Clear	Vague	Extremely vague
Explains in detail where you presently are	4	3	2	1
Explores your competitive environment	4	3	2	1
Is based on what is really happening now	4	3	2	1
Describes the goals in simple language	4	3	2	1
Discusses implementation	4	3	2	1
Explains steps or pathways for achieving goals	4	3	2	1
Outlines potential 'roadblocks' or obstacles	4	3	2	1
Explains 'why' this strategy exists	4	3	2	1
Language used is inclusive of all stakeholders	4	3	2	1
You would know when goals were achieved	4	3	2	1
Score				
Total score				

The maximum possible score is 40. The minimum is 10. How did your strategy score?

What does this result tell you about the quality and focus of the strategy? What limitations can you see? What needs to be improved?

_____

_____

_____

_____

_____

_____

_____

_____

CASE STUDY: APPLE'S STRATEGY IN CHINA

For many years Apple had a minimal presence in China. When the iPhone was first released in 2007, there was no distributor in China. This was a deliberate strategy. Apple opened its first Apple store in Beijing in 2008 (just before the Olympics) and by 2009 Apple derived only 2 per cent of its profits in China.

So why did Apple delay its entry into the China market? Well, instead of entering all regions at once, it decided to wait until it could enter the market in a meaningful way. Instead of making cheaper products for the Chinese market as other tech companies had, Apple chose to wait until Chinese disposable income increased to levels where Chinese consumers could afford Apple's main products. These products came with great prestige, as they were exclusive and expensive.

In 2013 Apple reported first-quarter revenue in China of $6.83 billion. Apple has even suggested that China will eventually become their largest market. Late in 2013, Apple announced an upgraded iPhone 5s and a cheaper, 'low-end' 5c made from plastic. This 'cheaper' iPhone will still sell in China for well over 4,000 yuan, whereas a normal Chinese smartphone sells for as little as 600 yuan.

COACHING SESSION 34

Case study: reflection

Was this a result of good strategy or good luck? What do you think? Write down your thoughts about Apple's China strategy. What can we learn from Apple?

_____

_____

_____

_____

_____

_____

_____

_____

_____

_____

THINKING STRATEGY: STRATEGIC ANALYSIS

Strategic analysis is about analysing the strength of an organization's present position (where we are now) and understanding the significant external factors that may influence that position. The process of strategic analysis can be assisted by a number of tools, including SWOT analysis, the Balanced Scorecard, PEST analysis, Directional Policy Matrix, Scenario Planning, USP analysis, Boston Matrix, Competitor analysis, Hoshin Planning System, Value Chain analysis, War Gaming and Five Forces analysis.

It is hard to believe that there are so many different tools (and I've listed only the best known). All of these tools have their place in strategic analysis. But for our purposes I am going to focus on just two – SWOT analysis and PEST analysis – although, if you have time (and the inclination), I recommend reading up on Porter's Five Forces model (Porter 1980) and the Balanced Scorecard (Kaplan & Norton 1992).

SWOT analysis

A SWOT analysis is a simple but widely used tool that helps in understanding the strengths, weaknesses, opportunities and threats involved in a strategic decision. Normally, it involves a 2 × 2 matrix as shown in Figure 6.2 below. In particular, it looks at:

- internal strengths
- internal weaknesses
- opportunities in the external environment
- threats in the external environment.

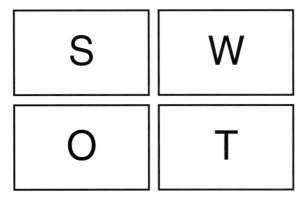

Figure 6.2 SWOT analysis

SWOT analysis is used primarily to assess the current position of an organization to determine a strategy for the future. It is a useful method of summarizing the key issues arising from an evaluation of an organization's 'internal' position and 'external' environmental influences. The following table shows the kind of questions you can ask when using the SWOT tool.

Strengths	Weakness
What your organization does well?	*Gaps in capabilities?*
Your unique selling points (USPs)?	*Cash flow, financials?*
Your competitive edge?	*Leadership?*
Resources, assets, people?	*Technology, innovation?*
Experience, reputation, culture, history?	*Human resources (people)?*
Opportunities	Threats
Gaps in the market?	*Competitors?*
Market developments?	*Technological change?*
Change (cultural, social, etc.)?	*Instability (markets, country, etc.)?*
New markets, vertical, horizontal?	*Economy - home, overseas?*
Partnerships, agencies, distribution?	*Seasonality, weather effects?*

 **ONLINE RESOURCE**

You can download the following SWOT analysis template by going to:

www.TYCoachbooks.com/Leadership

COACHING SESSION 35

SWOT analysis

Using the SWOT template below, conduct a SWOT analysis for a project or strategy that you know.

Strengths	Weakness

Opportunities	Threats

Conclusions

PEST ANALYSIS

PEST is an acronym for analysing the external macro-environment (Political, Economic, Sociological/demographic and Technological) and setting the stage for strategic planning. PEST analysis reviews the environment of a market and provides a snapshot of the external situation.

PEST factors are related to the opportunities or threats in a SWOT analysis.

Political factors	Economic factors
Government intervention	Economic growth
Employment/labour laws	Inflation rates
Ecological/environmental	Interest rates
Taxation policy	Exchange rates
Trade restrictions	Cost of capital
Political stability	Purchasing power
Wars and conflicts	Seasonality issues
Social factors	Technological factors
Demographics	Innovation
Ageing population	Automation
Attitude towards work	Rate of technological change
Heath issues	Research and development (R&D)
Consumer issues	Barriers to entry
Attitudes to safety	Technological incentives
Ethnic/religious factors	Licensing, patents, intellectual property

It is often useful to complete a PEST analysis before completing a SWOT analysis.

COACHING SESSION 36

PEST analysis

Using the PEST template below, conduct a PEST analysis for a project or strategy that you know well. Use the same one you used for the SWOT analysis or use a different one.

Political	Economic

Social	Technological

Conclusions

NEXT STEPS

In this chapter we have looked at the difficulties we face when we try to define strategy. We looked at how strategy can be applied to different levels of an organization and the value of having a clear strategy. Finally, we looked at two practical tools you can use to think about strategy: SWOT and PEST analysis.

In the next chapter we will look at the psychology and practice of motivation – what it is and how you can harness the power of motivation in your role as leader.

👍 TAKEAWAYS

Why is it difficult to simply define 'strategy'?

_____

_____

_____

_____

_____

_____

_____

_____

_____

How would you evaluate a strategy's clarity? What would you look for?

_____

_____

_____

_____

_____

_____

_____

_____

_____

_____

_____

_____

In what circumstances should you use a SWOT or a PEST analysis?

_____

_____

_____

_____

_____

_____

_____

_____

_____

_____

MOTIVATION

 OUTCOMES FROM THIS CHAPTER

- Learn how to motivate the people you lead and how to motivate yourself.
- Understand the three key theories of motivation that have 'real-world' application.
- Realize how rewarding employees for achieving can be much more effective than punishing them for failing.
- Learn how to set and achieve SMART goals in your work and home life.

'Nothing great was ever achieved without enthusiasm.'

Ralph Waldo Emerson

There is great variety in approaches to understanding motivation and a great deal of research has been carried out in this area. There is also an apparent lack of consensus among the major theorists, which results in the absence of a neat, workable theory. In some ways, this is not surprising as people are complex beings with a variety of changing, and often conflicting, needs, which they try to satisfy in a variety of ways.

WHAT IS MOTIVATION?

Motivation attempts to explain people's behaviour. There have been many attempts to define motivation and not all have been successful.

COACHING SESSION 37

Defining motivation

Why don't you have a go first? How would you define motivation?

_____

_____

_____

_____

_____

_____

_____

_____

_____

In simple terms, motivation is what drives or stimulates people to take certain actions or not to act. One useful definition is that motivation is 'a process in which people choose between alternative forms of behaviour in order to achieve personal goals' (Cole 2002). Some researchers define motivation as 'the reasons underlying behaviour' (Guay et al. 2010). Others suggest that it is about being 'pushed' or 'pulled' in a particular direction. Most researchers, however, agree that motivation is made up of three components:

1. **Direction:** what a person is trying to do or achieve

2. **Effort:** how hard a person is trying

3. **Persistence:** how long a person continues trying.

Deci & Ryan (1985) distinguish between different types of motivation based on the various goals. The most basic is between intrinsic motivation, which refers to doing something because it is inherently interesting or enjoyable, and extrinsic motivation, which refers to doing something because it leads to an external outcome.

⊕⊕ COACHING SESSION 38

Your definition

How does your definition above compare with these definitions?

_____

_____

_____

_____

_____

_____

_____

_____

_____

_____

_____

⊕⊕ COACHING SESSION 39

Personal motivation

Consider your personal motivation. What is it that makes you do things at work?

In the table below, create a list of those work activities in which you feel you perform well and those you could perform better in. Once you have completed that list, write down against each activity what it is that you think motivates you to perform and what is demotivating you.

Activities that I perform well:	What motivates or demotivates me about this activity?

Activities that I could perform better:	What motivates or demotivates me about this activity?

What does this list tell you about what motivates you? Do you think you are the same as other people? If so, why, and if not, why not?

_____

_____

_____

_____

_____

_____

_____

_____

_____

_____

_____

MOTIVATION THEORIES

Current theories of work motivation tend to split motivational factors into two parts: those factors that are intrinsic parts of the work (**content theories**) and those factors that address what makes motivation happen (**process theories**).

Consideration of theories of motivation can provide leaders with guidance for understanding motivation issues within their organization. There are dozens of motivational theories, and each is in its own way interesting. However, we will look briefly at four of the most relevant in relation to leadership and work motivation. These are:

- McGregor's Theory X and Theory Y
- Maslow's Hierarchy of Needs
- Herzberg's Motivation-hygiene Theory
- Locke's Goal Theory.

McGREGOR'S THEORY X AND THEORY Y

In 1960 Douglas McGregor published his book *The Human Side of Enterprise*. McGregor was interested in what motivated people, particularly in the workplace. He saw management thinking as being based on two different and somewhat opposing ideas, and he named these: 'Theory X' and 'Theory Y'.

Theory X

The traditional widely held view was labelled 'X'. It was based on the following assumptions:

- The average person has a dislike for work and will avoid it if they can.
- Because of this, most people must be coerced, directed or threatened to get them to work.
- Most people are not capable of imagination, resourcefulness and creativity.
- The average person prefers to be directed, avoid responsibility, has little ambition, and mainly values security.
- People are usually fully developed when they go to work and resist change.

While this view of workers was most characteristic of the first half of the twentieth century, it still exists today.

COACHING SESSION 40

Theory X

Assume you are a leader who believes in the Theory X approach to motivating staff. How might you go about motivating a team of people who are not performing well? Assume that you are their direct manager and remember that you believe that people are inherently lazy and undisciplined and need to be monitored closely.

You have a team of five people who have to produce an annual report by next week and they are two weeks behind in their work. What leadership techniques would you be most likely to apply as a Theory X leader?

The Theory X leader could demonstrate very contrasting styles of leadership. In this case, the leader may choose to drive people hard, based on a belief that people are inherently lazy and that this is the only way to guarantee performance. In this case, they may use threats, warnings or coercion to get the report done on time. Close monitoring and supervision would be high on the agenda. Another Theory X leader may look at people in the same way, but they may think that the way to get lazy people to work is to persuade them. So this leader may use rewards, praise or promises to get productivity from the annual report team.

Theory Y

Theory 'Y', in contrast to Theory X, is based on the following beliefs:

- Physical and intellectual effort at work is just as natural as play or rest.
- If people are committed to organizational objectives, they will work towards them. Commitment is dependent on rewards associated with self-respect and personal growth.
- People can learn, under proper conditions, not only to accept but to seek responsibility.
- Imagination, resourcefulness and creativity are widely, not narrowly, distributed.
- The intellectual potential of people is not fully utilized.

The focus of a Theory Y leader is on learning and development.

COACHING SESSION 41

Theory Y

Assume that you are a leader who believes in the Theory Y approach to motivating staff. How might you go about motivating the same team of people from Coaching session 40? Assume that you are their direct manager and remember that you believe that people will use self-direction and self-control in the service of objectives to which they are committed.

You have a team of five people who have to produce an annual report by next week and they are two weeks behind in their work. What leadership techniques would you be most likely to apply as a Theory Y leader?

_____

_____

_____

_____

_____

_____

_____

_____

_____

_____

_____

_____

_____

_____

_____

_____

_____

_____

_____

_____

_____

It is important to realize that Theory Y is not a 'soft' approach to leadership. It sets high standards and expects people to reach for them. Risk taking is necessary on the part of the leader, who must use and appreciate delegation. (See Chapter 2.)

In the above example, the Theory Y leader would first of all make sure that the team fully understands the objectives of the annual report and would then encourage them to discuss the importance of getting it done on time. In contrast to the Theory X leader, the Y leader would consider less observation and control. He or she would give people responsibility to encourage them to rise to the challenge. The emphasis would be on removing any existing barriers to the team's imagination, ingenuity and creativity.

It is relevant to note that McGregor realized that some of his theories might be unrealizable in practice, but he wanted leaders to examine their behaviours based on the two approaches.

COACH'S TIP

Getting Theory X right

- Giving workers more responsibility can make them rise to a challenge.

- Leaders must demonstrate trust for other people's work efforts.

- Motivation comes from the work itself and provides a much more powerful incentive than the 'externals' usually offered by the Theory X leader.

- Leaders need to work to remove any imposed barriers to workers' imagination and creativity.

- Rewarding employees for achieving can be much more effective than punishing them for failing.

COACHING SESSION 42

McGregor's Theory X and Theory Y

Can you think of any other tips from McGregor's theory? What implications does this have for you as a leader? Do you make the same assumptions about others that you make about yourself, and act in the appropriate manner?

MASLOW'S HIERARCHY OF NEEDS

Psychologist Abraham Maslow introduced his theory of motivation in his 1943 paper, 'A Theory of Human Motivation'. Maslow hypothesized that there is a progression where a person's needs are fulfilled in ascending order from the most undeveloped to the most advanced. His 'Hierarchy of Needs' is a very well-known theory. It is most often displayed as a pyramid, as can be seen in Figure 7.1.

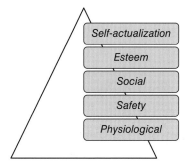

Figure 7.1 Maslow's Hierarchy of Needs (Maslow 1954)

Each level may be defined as follows:

- **Self-actualization:** growth, achieving one's potential and self-fulfilment

- **Esteem:** self-respect, autonomy, achievement, status and recognition

- **Social:** affection, belongingness, acceptance and friendship

- **Safety:** security and protection from physical and emotional harm

- **Physiological:** hunger, thirst, shelter, sex and other bodily needs.

According to Maslow, progression through the needs hierarchy is seen as a progression where the individual must have satisfied the lower level before moving up the pyramid. The knowledge of the need going higher up the pyramid is a function of having fulfilled the preceding need. Only satisfactory fulfilment of this need will enable the person to deal with the new need. According to Maslow, no need is ever completely satisfied; rather, there must be at least partial fulfilment before an individual can become aware of the higher-order need and be able to pursue it.

COACHING SESSION 43

Needs hierarchy

First, list the ten characteristics of your ideal job. Do this in the first column and don't worry about the second column at this stage.

Characteristics	Maslow's level
Example: lots of freedom	Esteem
1.	
2.	
3.	
4	
5.	
6.	
7.	
8.	
9.	
10.	

Now for each of your job characteristics, go back to your list and try to match them against the five Maslow levels above. What does this tell you about your own motivation?

_____

_____

_____

_____

_____

_____

_____

_____

Criticisms of Maslow's Hierarchy of Needs

Maslow's need hierarchy theory is well known, particularly among practising managers and corporate trainers. However, most psychological research has not been able to validate the idea of a needs hierarchy. Maslow himself provided no empirical substantiation for his theory and several studies that sought to validate his theory failed to do so. Maslow's research on self-actualization was based on a very small sample, including people he knew personally and on the written biographies of famous persons that Maslow himself believed to be self-actualized (e.g. Albert Einstein). He had great difficulty even writing a clear definition of 'self-actualization'.

There is little evidence to support Maslow's ranking of needs in the way he did and even less evidence that these needs are in a hierarchical order (Wahba & Bridwell 1976). For example, consider a person who is living in a refugee camp. This person has limited food and shelter (physiological needs not met), is in constant danger of attack or harm (no safety needs met) and may have lost all their family and friends when escaping persecution (social needs not met). Do you think it is possible for this person to have self-respect (esteem needs) or spiritual calm (self-actualization)? Of course they can: needs are not hierarchical; life is simply more complex than that.

The Indian business professor Anil Gupta, in an interesting TED Talk (2009), commented:

> 'There could be nothing more wrong than the Maslowian model of hierarchy of needs. ... Please do not ever think that only after meeting your physiological needs and other needs can you be thinking about your spiritual needs or your enlightenment.'

Regardless of these criticisms, Maslow's theory helped create an important shift in business psychology. Rather than focusing on abnormal behaviour, Maslow's theory was focused on the development of healthy individuals.

HERZBERG'S MOTIVATION-HYGIENE THEORY

The Motivation-Hygiene Theory was based on research collected from interviews with 203 engineers and accountants in the United States in the late 1950s by psychologist Frederick Herzberg. In establishing his theory, Herzberg draws heavily upon Maslow. He states that the factors which motivate people in organizations are the factors that give the worker a sense of personal accomplishment through the challenge of the work itself.

On the other hand, Herzberg maintains that environmental factors ('hygiene' factors) cause dissatisfaction when they are unhealthy. These dissatisfiers are felt only when they are absent. For example, good working conditions rarely motivate workers. However, bad working conditions will cause dissatisfaction.

This theory is also called the 'two-factor' theory as Herzberg compared two factors which he called 'motivators' and 'hygiene factors'. These can be seen in Figure 7.2 below.

Figure 7.2 Herzberg's Motivation-Hygiene Theory (Herzberg 1959)

An example of a 'hygiene factor' at work would be the employee who wants to be paid on time every fortnight so they can pay their bills. If the person is paid late, they would be really unhappy. But when they get paid on time every other fortnight they don't feel particularly motivated by being paid on time.

A further example of a 'motivator' might be the satellite dish installer who is given the list of places to cover during the day and asked to order them in the way he believes will be most efficient, rather than having been given an itinerary pre-planned by the manager who doesn't 'know the territory' first-hand as the installer does.

COACHING SESSION 44

Motivators and hygiene factors

Below is a table of some 'motivators' and 'hygiene factors'. I have given you five examples of each. Can you come up with at least another five for both 'motivators' and 'hygiene factors'?

Motivators (job content)	Hygiene factors (job environment)
Satisfiers	Dissatisfiers
Work itself	Company policy
Achievement	Supervision
Recognition	Working conditions
Responsibility	Salary
Growth	Administration

Here is a completed table – did your answers match any of them?

Motivators (job content)	Hygiene factors (job environment)
Satisfiers	Dissatisfiers
Work itself	Company policy
Achievement	Supervision
Recognition	Working conditions
Responsibility	Salary
Growth	Administration
Advancement	Fringe benefits
Opportunity to acquire authority	Rules and regulations
Decision-making authority	Company cars
Work matched to interests	Benefits
Praise from superiors	Bonuses
Interesting work	Status
Self-directed work	Job security
Tasks that 'stretch' you	Office life
Awards for service	Nice office environment

Motivators (job content)	Hygiene factors (job environment)
Meeting or exceeding set goals	Free refreshments
Self-directed/managed teams	Office parties
Coaching	Work–life balance
Mentoring	Holidays
Some training	Some training
Appraisal focused on development	Appraisal focused on salary
Promotion	Facilities available
Progress in the organization	Travel time to work
Temporary 'growth' assignments	Working hours
That advancement is possible	Subsidized or free meals
Work aligned to personal values	Employee counselling (EAP)
Autonomous work systems	Massage service at work
Talent management strategies	Concierge services
Succession planning	Health care
Career planning	Environmental policies

CASE STUDY: ROBBIE

Robbie ran a small but successful computer animation company. He had five key computer designers working for him and he wanted to keep them motivated and happy. He visited a computer products trade show and was excited to see a unique high-tech ergonomic operator's chair. It was like something from *Star Trek* and he knew that his team would be excited by them. But each chair cost £3,000. Nevertheless, he ordered five of them. 'This will really motivate them; I bet I get back my money fivefold in increased productivity,' he thought.

The designers were delighted with the high-tech chairs, but after a few months Robbie was worried. He hadn't seen any real increase in productivity; no one was putting in extra hours, and the designers even seemed blasé about the new chairs. He began to question his purchase: was it a waste of money?

⚆⚆ COACHING SESSION 45

Case study: reflection

So what does Herzberg's theory tell us about Robbie's decision to buy the chairs? Would a great office chair be a motivator or a hygiene factor? Did Robbie spend his money wisely? What else could he have done?

_____

_____

_____

_____

_____

_____

_____

_____

_____

_____

_____

_____

_____

_____

Robbie made the mistake of confusing motivators with hygiene factors. The expensive high-tech office chairs were definitely hygiene factors. So they would have prevented dissatisfaction but not necessarily motivated any of his computer designers. People would have been happy with the new chairs, but that happiness would have been short-lived and unlikely to lead to increased work or effort from the team. The purchase might still have been wise: the ergonomic and occupational health benefits could be great (fewer sore backs and lost days) and may be a good long-term investment. However, if Robbie truly wanted to motivate his team, he should have considered different things.

Robbie needs to:

- examine the work of his designers to see how it could be made better and more satisfying to each designer
- consider providing opportunities for achievement
- make sure that he is recognizing each designer's contributions
- ensure that the work matches the skills and abilities of each worker.

Could he give some of the designers more responsibility? Are there opportunities to advance in the business? What learning and development opportunities does he offer?

You can probably see how Herzberg-type motivators might have cost a lot less than five £3,000 chairs. So Robbie, by applying the Herzberg theories, might find that spending his money on something else was a better long-term investment in his people.

To apply Herzberg's theory in your own organization, you need first to eliminate dissatisfactions. For example, can you improve the work environment, increase salaries to an equitable level, or ensure that you have good human resource policies in place?

The second step is to help people find satisfaction. This could be done in many ways, but you should focus on areas such as increasing people's responsibility, providing opportunities for growth and making sure that people are fully recognized for the good work they do. If you truly want to motivate people, give praise wherever and whenever you can.

Criticisms of Herzberg

Unlike Maslow, who offered little research to support his theory, Herzberg's two-factor theory has extensive empirical evidence to support it. However, some researchers have criticized the method that Herzberg used in his research and questioned the reliability of his methodology.

 COACH'S TIP

Getting Herzberg right

- People are made dissatisfied by a bad environment, but they are seldom made satisfied by a good environment.
- There is nothing more important in motivation that recognizing and praising good work.
- Any result from hygiene factors (such as bonuses and salary increases) will be limited and temporary.
- If you can, offer people plenty of options when using hygiene factors.
- Make sure you communicate with people regularly to find out what motivates them.

LOCKE'S GOAL THEORY

The psychologist Edwin Locke conducted groundbreaking research on motivation in the late 1960s. According to his theory, people who have challenging but achievable goals perform better than those who have less challenging goals.

Locke found that performance is maximized by setting:

- clear and specific goals rather than no goals or 'do your best' goals
- difficult but attainable goals rather than easy goals.

Multiple reviews and meta-analyses of the goal-setting literature have concluded that there is substantial support for the fundamental principles of goal-setting theory (Ambrose & Kulik 1999). In their comprehensive review of the goal-setting literature, Locke & Latham (1990) reported that approximately 400 studies using more than 40,000 subjects have shown that specific, challenging goals lead to better performance than specific, easy goals.

Based on Locke's ideas, it is helpful to use the well-known acronym SMART when constructing goals. The widely used SMART tool was introduced by George Doran in an article in 1981:

S	Specific	The more clearly you can specify a goal the better (who, what, where, etc.).
M	Measurable	Have quantitative and qualitative criteria for your goal.
A	Attainable	Although goals should stretch you into new areas, they should be realistic.
R	Relevant	Goals should matter – link your goal to a higher-level goal, if possible.
T	Time-bound	Set yourself a deadline – create a sense of urgency.

Some writers have even added 'E' and 'R' to the end (SMARTER goals). These additional letters can stand for various things (Enlist, Energize, Ethical, Enthusiasm) and (Re-evaluate, Real, Recorded, Rewarding). However, these extra letters do not add anything significant to the established SMART mnemonic.

COACHING SESSION 46

Goal setting

In the table below, set yourself one 'work' and one 'non-work' (home) goal for the short, medium and long term.

	Work goal	Home goal
Short term (1–3 weeks)		
Medium term (1–3 months)		
Long term (1–3 years)		

Now, choose one of the six goals you have identified above and use the SMART template below to expand on it in more detail.

S	*Specific* Write a specific goal over and against a more general one. The more clearly you can specify a goal the better (consider: who, what, where, when).	
M	*Measurable* Use concrete criteria for measuring progress toward the attainment of the goal. Try to have quantitative and qualitative criteria so you know when the goal is met.	
A	*Attainable* Set goals that are realistic and attainable (but challenging). Although goals should stretch you into new areas, they should be realistic.	
R	*Relevant* Always choose goals that matter – that are worthwhile. Try to connect your goal to a higher-level goal if possible (such as an organizational goal).	
T	*Time-bound* Ground goals within a timeframe, giving them a clear and specific target date. The 'due date' can create a very useful sense of urgency.	

ONLINE RESOURCE

You can download the SMART templates in this coaching session by going to:

www.TYCoachbooks.com/Leadership

NEXT STEPS

In this chapter we have looked at the area of motivation. We saw how motivation is a very complex area of human behaviour as people are very complex beings, often with conflicting and confusing needs. However, an understanding of motivation is necessary for any leader who wants to get the best out of people.

We have seen how three key theories of motivation can help us as a leader and how these theories of motivation complement each other. The three theories presented here are not all the important ideas available on motivation. If you are particularly interested in this area you should have a look at McClelland's Learned Needs Theory (Achievement Motivation); Alderfer's ERG Theory; Adams' Equity Theory (Justice Theory); Vroom's Expectancy Theory; and Cognitive Evaluation Theory (CET). Some references to these theories are provided in the reference section at the end of this workbook.

In the next chapter we will look at the significant area of conflict management. This chapter explores workplace conflict from an experiential perspective and seeks to explain how a reframing of our understanding of conflict can help us to create a framework for responding to and managing workplace conflict that is empowering and transformative for individuals and organizations.

TAKEAWAYS

Does motivation come from within a person, or is it a result of the situation? Why?

_____

_____

_____

_____

_____

_____

_____

_____

_____

_____

_____

_____

How does Maslow's Hierarchy of Needs theory compare with Herzberg's two-factor theory?

_____

_____

_____

_____

_____

_____

_____

_____

_____

_____

_____

_____

_____

_____

You join an organization as the new leader. The staff work in an old, unattractive building with a terrible heating system. The work itself is tedious and the direct manager is rarely available. You have decided to try to apply Herzberg's two-factor theory to the situation. What will you do first?

_____

_____

_____

_____

_____

_____

_____

_____

_____

_____

MANAGING WORKPLACE CONFLICT

OUTCOMES FROM THIS CHAPTER

- Realize that conflict is an important and necessary part of life.
- Understand that conflict can be both constructive and destructive.
- Learn how to reframe your perception of conflict.

'Everything that irritates us about others can lead us to an understanding of ourselves.'

Carl Jung

According to the *Oxford English Reference Dictionary* (1995), conflict is 'a serious disagreement or argument, typically a protracted one'. Conflict can occur whenever there is a high level of interdependence or when people have different values, or if resources are scarce and people are under stress or facing an uncertain environment.

COACHING SESSION 47

Defining conflict

When you hear the word 'conflict', what words or pictures come to mind? Write them down now.

What sort of words did you list above? *Opposition, hostilities, fighting, struggle, contradictory, incompatible, war, violence, shouting?* In fact, most people, when they think of conflict, automatically consider it a 'bad' thing, as something to be avoided. However, this negative view of conflict is very limited. It is much better to consider conflict as *both* destructive and constructive.

How can conflict be considered a good thing? Have a look at the table below. Here you can see how conflict can be positive and negative, constructive and destructive.

Constructive (positive) conflict	Destructive (negative) conflict
More creative thinking – conflict is often at the root of creativity.	Conflict can destroy a group and a sense of 'we'.
When people have worked through conflict, you often get greater commitment to any decisions.	Conflict leads to stalemates – where both sides won't 'give an inch'.
Allowing conflict to happen can create a free and open atmosphere.	Conflict can destroy relationships – even strong, long-term ones.
Conflict can lead to better-quality decisions – there is less 'groupthink'.	Someone wins, but someone loses.
Conflict challenges the status quo – a good thing in all organizations.	Conflict can result in expensive litigation and major hostilities.

If asked to describe what constitutes workplace conflict, most of us would initially associate the word 'conflict' with experiences in our present or past working life that were negative, stressful or distressing. Those situations would most likely be characterized by a sense of frustration and powerlessness, and this would be true irrespective of whether you are in the role of a leader, manager or team member (Buon 2008).

We would no doubt also be able to recall positive experiences of open communication where we felt heard and understood in the process of resolving our conflicts at work. These positive experiences of conflict would be characterized by a sense of shared power, trust and mutual respect, even though we may not always have achieved our preferred outcome.

In this sense, our experience of workplace conflict is not unlike our experience of conflict in our personal and family lives, in that, while we do have significant and rewarding experiences of being able to work through our conflicts with each other, we still tend to have an overriding perception of conflict as something undesirable, negative and difficult to deal with.

CASE STUDY: ALAN AND BILL

Alan feels belittled by the way one of his colleagues, Bill, always criticizes his ideas and input in front of the rest of the department at their monthly meetings. He believes that it will only make things worse if he says something about it as this will make him look 'thin-skinned' and 'weak', neither of which he feels are 'tolerated' in his organization. He has therefore decided just to 'put up with it', even though he can feel his confidence to speak up at meetings is all but gone (Buon 2008).

COACHING SESSION 48

Case study: reflection (I)

Why do you think Alan has decided to avoid the conflict with Bill?

_____

_____

_____

_____

_____

_____

_____

_____

_____

_____

_____

_____

_____

_____

_____

What would you do in this situation?

_____

_____

_____

_____

_____

_____

_____

_____

_____

_____

_____

Alan's decision to use avoidance as a way of dealing with this situation is underpinned by a number of powerful beliefs:

- He believes that Bill's actions are belittling.

- He believes that communicating openly about the situation will make him vulnerable and worsen the situation.

- He believes that neither his managers nor the organization will understand or support his concerns.

Ultimately, it is Alan's belief that dealing with the situation would result in a negative conflict and it is his desire to avoid that conflict that governs how he perceives his options for action. Perhaps even more important is the way in which this belief system is also a determinant of how the situation will evolve as it continues to affect his sense of wellbeing at work and his ability to perform and make a contribution at work.

It is clear that in this instance the absence or avoidance of conflict between Alan and Bill is not contributing to the organization's function or the wellbeing of its employees.

♀♀ COACHING SESSION 49

Case study: reflection (II)

What do you think caused this problem in the first place?

_____

_____

_____

_____

_____

_____

_____

_____

_____

_____

_____

_____

_____

There are many personal and organizational precursors or contributing factors in the development of workplace conflict. The point at which a given person will feel a particular intensity of internal response to a conflict will vary. A conflict situation or issue that appears trivial or inconsequential to one person may evoke intense feelings of anger, betrayal, injustice or hurt in another person. It is also very common for one party to feel distressed by something that is happening and for the other person to be unaware of this.

In Alan and Bill's case we can see that this is what has occurred: Alan has not spoken with Bill about the way his behaviour is making him feel and it may well be that Bill is completely unaware of the impact that his behaviour is having on his colleague.

COACHING SESSION 50

Conflict factors

Have a look at the table below. Which factors do you think could be responsible for the conflict in Alan and Bill's case? Can you add anything to the list?

Individual factors	✓	Organizational factors	✓
Poor communication skills		Lack of leadership	
Diversity and differences		Office politics	
Competing needs and goals		Inappropriate management style	
Past experiences of conflict		Poor work performance systems	
Lack of negotiation skills		'Blame and shame' workplace culture	
Personal problems outside work		Overly competitive workplace culture	
Conflicting values and principles		Physical environment	
Inappropriate use of power		Scarce resources	
Lack of job satisfaction		Lack of recognition	
Fear		Inflexible working practices	
Workload		Workload	
Lack of autonomy		Poor morale	
Cultural issues		Cultural issues	
Inability to make choices		Unfair decision-making practices	
Being in the wrong job		Lack of organizational due process	
Internal emotional states		Lack of clarity about roles	
Low self-esteem		Job design	
Language difficulties		Lack of job security	
Relationship problems		Unrealistic expectations	
Physical or mental health problems		Power distribution	
Alcohol or other drug-related problems		Over-reliance on email rather than face-to-face communication	
Concern over shame (loss of face)		Promotion on technical knowledge alone	
Underdeveloped emotional competencies		Ineffective conflict resolution processes	
Misperceptions and misunderstandings		Incomplete briefings and/or delegation	
Lack of assertiveness skills		Lack of training and development	

Individual factors	✓	Organizational factors	✓

THE NATURE OF WORKPLACE CONFLICT

In reality, an employee's experience of workplace conflict can be both negative and positive and the factors that contribute to whether it is one or the other or a mixed experience are complex and multifaceted.

While such individual responses to a given situation vary greatly, in general terms it is known that situations involving inherent human needs such as individual and group identity, recognition, or developmental needs tend to evoke powerful emotions. It is these unmet or unrecognized human needs that underpin intensely felt conflict situations. At the core of such conflicts, a person may experience a sense of threat to their identity and begin to experience significant symptoms of distress or stress.

In any conflict situation, there will be elements of both unmet human needs and the material or negotiable issues. As a conflict becomes more intensely felt over time, the challenge in creating a resolution is to assess these elements as accurately as possible and then to adopt the most appropriate approach that addresses both of these aspects.

☺☺ COACHING SESSION 51

Personal conflict situation table

Think about a recent conflict in your life (work or private). Complete the table below, taking into account everything you know about the situation.

Situation (Describe briefly.)			
Who is involved? (all parties)			
When did this conflict start?			
How do the parties say it started?			
What causes can you identify? (Use the table in Coaching session 50 above.)			

There is a whole range of behaviours that may contribute to the evolution of workplace conflict. In any work group or team, such behaviours will always arise and will vary in intensity and duration, depending upon:

- the nature of the conflict

- the make-up of the individuals

- the collective history of the group or team and the skills and experience of the leaders and others intervening in the conflict situation

- the wider culture of the organization.

While the conflict may start at one end of this continuum, involving behaviours that are seemingly minor or that can reasonably be regarded as just a normal part of day-to-day working life, minor conflict situations have the potential to change or 'metamorphose' (Fortado 2001) into far more serious conflicts involving behaviours such as bullying or harassment, sabotage, physical assault or violence.

If a conflict is not managed through effective early intervention, or if it is mishandled, then the potential for this type of metamorphosis to occur increases, especially where the conflict centres on unmet human needs and where a high level of emotional intensity for one or more of the individuals is present.

In Figure 8.1, the wavy line indicates that it is extremely difficult, if not impossible, to pinpoint or predict the exact point at which this change will occur.

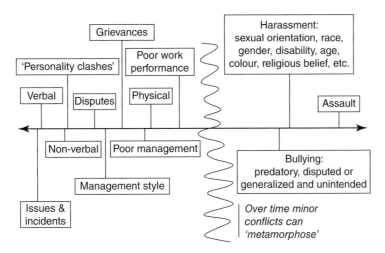

Figure 8.1 Continuum of behaviour (Buon 2008)

CASE STUDY: CLAIRE

Claire was part of a team of specialist assessors working in a large insurance company. She had been in the job for a couple of years and was on her way to becoming a senior assessor. Until then, she still needed to collaborate very closely with her colleagues in order to have certain reports signed off before they could be completed. Claire was very committed to her work but had a tendency to divert from procedures. The team of assessors was a very tight-knit group at work and socially, but Claire was never really brought into the social group as she was seen to be a bit snobbish and often made remarks about topics at the lunch table that the rest of the group did not agree with and found off-putting.

Claire's supervisor, Stefan, was very close to the rest of his team and also had a problem warming to Claire and did not really like her. Claire felt increasingly excluded from the group and when Stefan or the other team members needed to speak with Claire about her job performance they were met by very emotional and defensive responses. Finally, Claire's work performance began to suffer further, as she became more and more distressed at work.

Finding the situation intolerable, Claire went off on stress leave and brought a formal grievance against her supervisor and other team members for bullying and victimization. After a formal investigation, the grievance was not upheld and Claire took the matter to the appeal stage where, once again, it was not upheld. She did not return from sick leave and eventually made a claim for constructive dismissal, which resulted in a compromise agreement before it went to a tribunal hearing (Buon 2008).

COACHING SESSION 52

Case study: reflection

What do you think were the factors that contributed to the way in which this relatively minor conflict changed or metamorphosed into a grievance about bullying?

The factors that contributed to the way in which this relatively minor conflict changed or metamorphosed into a grievance about bullying can be summarized as follows:

- Claire was not finding it easy to be accepted by the group.

- Claire had some issues with her job performance that needed to be addressed by her supervisor.

- Stefan and the team did not like Claire and did not feel comfortable letting her into their social group.

- When the job performance issues were raised with Claire, she overreacted because she was feeling distressed about her sense of exclusion from the group.

- Claire's overreaction reinforced the group's belief that Claire was a 'difficult' person to work with.

- Stefan was unable to maintain proper boundaries between his friendship with colleagues and his role as a line manager and so did not provide an equal level of support to Claire.

The dynamic in this team was clearly a very significant factor underlying the way in which this conflict escalated into a formal grievance.

For Claire, what started as a feeling of not fitting in with and being accepted by the group eventually metamorphosed into a much more powerful sense of being victimized and excluded. In this sense, her identity within the group was at stake, and it is this powerful unmet human need that intensified and escalated the conflict for her.

For the group, their belief that Claire was not a good fit within their team created a sense of threat to the established group identity and so they saw it as a failure on Claire's part to do what was needed to 'fit in', as opposed to anything they were saying or doing that prevented her from being a part of the group.

In addition, the way in which the situation was handled by the supervisor did nothing to change this dynamic or to prevent the escalation of the conflict within the team, as Stefan was a part of that same group dynamic. In all likelihood, had he been able to maintain appropriate boundaries and provide support to all of his team members and manage Claire's job performance appropriately, this team would have learned some valuable lessons about the diversity of approaches and personalities within a team and Claire would not have lost her job.

COACHING SESSION 53

Functional conflict

Now return to your 'personal conflict situation' table begun in Coaching session 51 and complete the section below.

Situation (Describe briefly.)	
Is this conflict constructive or destructive?	
What can this conflict situation tell me about myself, my working relationships, my team or my organization?	

RESOURCES FOR RESPONDING TO CONFLICT

An individual's or organization's capacity to respond effectively and positively to conflict is dependent upon the internal personal and organizational resources available to create and support that response. The following list provides a brief overview of some of the key resources that are utilized in response to workplace conflict.

- **Self-awareness:** As we have already seen, understanding yourself and your personal 'triggers' can be a very valuable resource in understanding conflict and the impact it has on you. Self-awareness allows you to understand other people, how they perceive you, and your responses to them in any conflict situation.

- **Resilience:** Resilience is that indefinable quality that allows some people to experience a problem and come back stronger than ever. Some of the factors that contribute to resilience are: a positive attitude, optimism and the ability to regulate emotions. Resilience is a skill and, as with all skills, you can develop it. When faced with a conflict situation, learn from the experience and next time you will be better equipped.

- **Social and interpersonal skills:** Active listening skills, an understanding of non-verbal communication and the ability to remove barriers to communication (see Chapter 4) can all assist you in resolving work and personal conflict situations.

- **Leader intervention:** The employment relationship has an inherent power imbalance and so all employees need to know that natural justice is enshrined in an organization's policies, procedures and in leadership behaviour. Your intervention as a leader should be perceived as equitable, fair, visible and consistently applied to all.

- **Mediation schemes:** Mediation is the intervention into a conflict situation by a third party. This person usually has no decision-making powers but simply assists the parties in conflict to resolve the issues they are facing. Mediation is a very effective *informal* process, and many companies and organizations are now establishing workplace mediation schemes.

- **Policies and procedures:** It is essential to have in place a robust and meaningful set of complaint or grievance-handling procedures as this forms the baseline for the way in which organizational due process is communicated and managed within an organization.

- **Employee assistance or welfare support:** As conflict can be rooted in personal problems (or can cause personal problems), it is important to have resources such as an Employee Assistance Programme (EAP) available for staff. These EAPs usually offer free, professional counselling for all employees and their families for all types of problems.

Clearly, there is no one correct way to respond to all workplace conflict as each conflict situation will present its own unique set of issues and challenges. There must then be an ability to be flexible and adaptable if our responses and interventions are going to be consistently effective.

COACHING SESSION 54

Resolving conflict

Now return to your 'personal conflict situation' table begun in Coaching sessions 51 and 53 and complete the section below.

Situation (Describe briefly.)	
Assess your response to the conflict situation	Is the conflict constructive or destructive?
	What are the sources/causes?
	Do the conditions exist for resolution – opportunity, capacity, willingness?
	What are the best methods for handling the conflict – informal or formal?

What resources for responding to conflict are available? (See list above.)			
From this list, which is your preferred option?			
What is the preferred option for the other party or parties?			
What is your next step? (Are there any barriers still stopping you from attempting to resolve this?)			

Now have a go at trying to resolve the conflict!

 ONLINE RESOURCE

You can download the complete 'personal conflict situation' template by going to:

www.TYCoachbooks.com/Leadership

→ NEXT STEPS

In this chapter we have looked at conflict and how as a leader you must work proactively at creating an environment within which people feel encouraged to take responsibility for creating solutions and feel safe enough to communicate openly about what the real issues are. It must also be a place where individuals are encouraged to learn and grow through conflict and so feel empowered to transform their problems into a way forward.

In the next chapter we will look at how to lead and manage change in an organization. The management of change has become a major preoccupation for leaders and change management has been said to explain the real essence of a leader's role. No matter what activities a leader becomes involved in, from striving to implement strategy to making simple amendments to a policy, all of these activities require change-management skills and knowledge to achieve the change effectively.

👍 TAKEAWAYS

In your own words, write down some definitions of negative and positive conflict.

_____

_____

_____

_____

_____

_____

_____

_____

_____

_____

_____

What tools can you use to resolve conflict?

_____

_____

_____

_____

_____

_____

_____

_____

_____

_____

_____

_____

With regard to your 'personal conflict situation' above, did you try to resolve the conflict? What happened? What could have been done better?

_____

_____

_____

_____

_____

_____

_____

_____

_____

LEADING CHANGE

9

 OUTCOMES FROM THIS CHAPTER

- Understand the importance of managing change effectively.
- Consider the impact of change on organizations and individuals.
- Understand how approaches to change management need to take into account the individual.
- Learn how the 'Five Phases of Change' model can serve as a useful diagnostic tool to support and lead people.

'Everything flows and nothing abides. Everything gives way and nothing stays fixed.'

Heraclitus of Ephesus

The leadership of change has become a major preoccupation for leaders and, no matter what activities a leader becomes involved in, all of these activities require change-management skills. Every time a leader makes a decision, some type of change occurs.

While understanding the key drivers of change and their effects on organizations is necessary, leaders also need to understand the key influences that will determine the success of any change initiative. Organizations are made up of human beings and an understanding of how people react psychologically to change is a necessary prerequisite for effective leadership.

Change is a fact of life in all organizations. There are different levels of change, which range all the way from a minor alteration in a work procedure to a major overhaul of organizational structure.

In exploring the techniques of managing change, it is necessary to understand the different characteristics of change and the impact of change on both the organization and individuals. Most people would suggest that significant or dramatic changes are the most complicated to handle, but experience shows that even simple changes can produce complex, and sometimes costly, consequences.

COACHING SESSION 55

An experience of change

Think about a change that you have experienced either in your private life, at work or in any organization with which you have been involved. Describe what the change was and how you, as an individual, felt about the change.

_____

_____

_____

_____

_____

_____

_____

_____

_____

_____

CASE STUDY: THE WATER COOLERS

Elaine is the new director of a small but thriving organization. The Board has told her that her first task is to cut costs. So, after looking over the accounts (and after nearly falling over dozens of empty containers), she decides to reduce the number or water coolers in the office from three to one. This is a small thing, but Elaine feels that it sends the right message and saves a little needed cash. The response from the team is instantaneous and fierce. People are upset and angry: comments include, 'Well, this shows what they think of us!', 'What's next – salaries?' and 'She is penny pinching – but I bet she didn't take a cut in her package.' One staff member even tells her manager that she is sure that this is a sign that the organization is going out of business and that she is looking for a new job.

Did people overreact? Possibly, but this is a good example of how a relatively minor change, which was designed to reduce costs and improve storage space, can have a disproportionate effect on staff. It is therefore necessary, before engaging in any form of change initiative, to fully analyse the results and outcomes of the proposed change.

COACHING SESSION 56

Case study: reflection

What could Elaine have done to analyse the characteristics and consequences of her proposed change?

_____

_____

_____

_____

_____

_____

_____

_____

_____

_____

_____

_____

_____

_____

_____

_____

_____

CHANGE AT THE PERSONAL LEVEL

Unless the person has a considerable impact on the performance of an organization, changes at the individual level do not usually have significant implications for an organization. Exceptions, of course, would be where perhaps a key technical specialist leaves or a new managing director is appointed.

If, however, we think of an organization as a system of interrelated departments or processes, we can see how change at the individual level, particularly if the change is significant, can impact upon the whole organization. No matter how simple or inconsequential the change may appear to be, the further and wider ramifications of that change must always be considered.

CHANGE AT THE TEAM LEVEL

In terms of their impact, changes at the team level can have a significant impact on organizations. The simple reason for this is that today most organizations are made up of teams or groups.

Changes at the team level can affect workflow, communications, job design, social relationships and the power structures within an organization. While these changes might be driven in a planned way, the impact of the reaction to change from teams and other informal groups should not be ignored.

CHANGE AT THE ORGANIZATIONAL LEVEL

Overall organizational change is often referred to as 'organizational development' (OD) and the management of change is a significant part of the OD process.

Decisions regarding change are generally made by an organization's leadership. The implementations of any proposed changes are seldom the responsibility of an individual person and are more usually organization-wide initiatives. Such initiatives take place over extended time frames, as they could include such things as a major restructuring of the organization, events such as a merger or acquisition or the major refocusing of the organization's strategy (see Chapter 6).

CASE STUDY: NOKIA AND MICROSOFT

In 2013 Nokia Corporation, a Finnish multinational, agreed to sell its mobile phone business to Microsoft for £4.6 ($7.6) billion. Nokia shares soared at the news, whereas Microsoft's fell. The deal was seen as an attempt to save Nokia and, for Microsoft, to get properly into the smartphone market dominated by Google's Android-based phones and Apple's iPhone. The purchase was scheduled to be completed in early 2014, when more than 30,000 Nokia employees would move to Microsoft. Nokia CEO Stephen Elop was due to become the Executive VP of the Microsoft Devices and Services unit.

COACHING SESSION 57

Case study: reflection

What impact do you think this change will have on both organizations? Consider the impact at all three levels – individual, group and organizational.

Impact of change

	Nokia	Microsoft
Individual level		
Group level		
Organizational level		

THE KEY DRIVERS OF CHANGE

Change is happening in all organizations, and every sector is, to a greater or lesser extent, affected by change. Change may seem to be a modern phenomenon but changes have occurred throughout the history of humankind.

> *'There is nothing more difficult to take in hand, more perilous to conduct, or more uncertain in its success than to take the lead in the introduction of a new order of things, because the innovator has for enemies all those who have done well under the old conditions, and lukewarm defenders in those who may do well under the new.'*

Niccolò Machiavelli, *The Prince* (1513)

Machiavelli's view is as relevant today as it was in 1513. Human beings continue to dislike change and today the rate of change is accelerating. Recent events would echo this: it used to take years to fight a war; now it takes days. To begin to manage change, it may first be helpful to try to define what change is and what factors drive change.

Change can come in many and varied forms – from, at one extreme, cataclysmic world events to, at the other extreme, a simple adjustment to a filing system. However, no matter how large or small the change is, the same dynamics are present and the same set of leadership skills are needed to manage the change or cope with the results of the change.

In your organizational life, you will have seen and probably experienced changes in technology, shifts in competition, takeovers and mergers, 'downsizing' and moves towards more flexible styles of working.

COACHING SESSION 58

Change in our world

Think about those factors that influence change in the world. Now list five of those factors that you think have been the most influential in the last 25 years.

1 _____

2 _____

3 _____

4 _____

5 _____

COACHING SESSION 59

Drivers of change

What are the key drivers for change in your work or profession? List them below and comment briefly on the impact that they have had.

Key drivers	Impact
e.g. digital technology	e.g. I no longer need to know how to develop photographic film.

CHANGE MANAGEMENT

Despite there being several models of change management, there is no comprehensive model that can be applied to all circumstances. Some writers suggest that the essential factors for successful change are in the consideration of vision, mission, culture, communications and leadership. Others suggest that, in addition to these, the identification of long- and short-term objectives and the strategies for implementing and consolidating the change are critical success factors.

In an attempt to reconcile these various views, I would suggest that the following points are the most frequently occurring themes:

- establishing a clear vision for the future

- carrying out a 'Present Position Audit'

- identifying measurable objectives for the change with long- and short-term goals

- establishing firm leadership for the change.

Establishing a clear vision for the future

The development of a clear vision of the future sets the direction for a change initiative and facilitates the establishment of the change objectives. When you establish an organization's vision, it needs to be clear and unambiguous. If the vision is unclear, the change objectives will similarly lack clarity.

Carrying out a 'Present Position Audit'

Many commentators suggest that the process of change is much like a journey with a defined start and finish point and a series of critical 'milestones' on the way. It is necessary to know where you are going with the change, but, of equal importance, you need to understand the current condition of your organization. There are number of analytical tools that have been developed to assist with this process and they include SWOT analysis and PEST analysis (see Chapter 6).

Identifying the change objectives

The identification of the change objectives and the long- and short-term goals allows resource needs to be identified and allows for measurement of the progress of the change initiative. Your objectives should be challenging but realistic, and you should express your objectives in terms that are measurable, so that you can tell when you have achieved them. Also, consider carefully how you intend to communicate your goal to all those directly involved in the change and to those who may be affected by it.

Leadership and change

With change approaching organizations from many different directions and with ever-increasing speed, it is essential for leaders to both effectively react to the needs of change and proactively look for the critical signs of approaching change. Effective information gathering and analysis therefore become crucial leadership skills and research becomes an important factor when planning change. Organizations that can identify impending change through observing and analysing trends in their operating environment are those that are most likely to achieve change successfully.

COACHING SESSION 60

Leadership and change

Consider a change that has taken place in your organization or in another organization with which you are familiar, and assess how organizational leadership managed the change. What did they do well? What could have been done better?

_____

_____

_____

_____

_____

_____

_____

_____

_____

'PEOPLE FACTORS' THAT INFLUENCE THE CHANGE PROCESS

In spite of the wealth of literature available on organizational change that leaders can draw on, we know that the majority of change initiatives fail. The reason for this is the failure by leaders to take on board the 'people factors', which can in the long run be critical to the success or failure of change initiatives. Research indicates that too much attention is given to process issues, such as changing structures and systems, at the expense of the people factors.

The failure to communicate the need, or make the case for change, can result in employees not fully understanding why the change is necessary or even result in suspicion or lack of trust, to the extent that employees may believe that information is deliberately being withheld or distorted. Leaders also often fail to take account of individual differences. For example, some people are able to cope with change and others are not. In the latter case, the need for support, communication and direct intervention by managers in the form of counselling (EAP) or training might be needed

Many of the reasons for employees' resistance to change and the lack of success of change initiatives are explained by the failure to deal adequately with the psychological pressures that change stimulates. Research has identified five psychological responses to change and these are detailed below, together with appropriate management strategies.

THE FIVE PHASES OF CHANGE

In the early 1960s the psychologist Elisabeth Kübler-Ross undertook research into how people came to terms with change. Her research involved the investigation of the stages and behaviours displayed when coming to terms with terminal illness (Kübler-Ross 1969).

Her research identified that a person facing death or bereavement goes through a number of steps after the initial shock in order to accept the situation. Subsequent studies established that people go through very similar stages when any significant change takes place in their life, and this extends to the work situation. For example, when an individual experiences the loss of their job, being moved to another location, or even accepts a promotion, they go through these same stages. If managers are aware of the psychological phases, and can identify which phase particular group members have reached, they can adapt their response to take the most appropriate action and provide support and advice.

The five phases or 'coping mechanisms' are:

1. **Denial:** An initial response to a significant personal change is to deny the event. It is not uncommon for individuals who have just been made redundant to deny that the event has happened. Similarly, on being promoted, someone may, for a time, carry on as if little has changed.

2. **Anger:** This can manifest itself in different ways. If the change is not initiated by the person themselves, the anger can be very strong. Often, people at this stage do not know who to blame and will vent their frustration on anyone who happens to be around at the time.

3. **Bargaining:** This is a common response but rarely provides a workable solution. Kübler-Ross found that people facing death often at this stage attempt to bargain with God. A person being forced to transfer may try to negotiate staying in their present location. Guilt is also common here. For example, someone may feel guilty about having *not* lost their job in a 'downsizing'.

4. **Depression:** Following the initial shock of the change, there is a period of sadness and depression. There can also be a feeling of helplessness. If someone has found their work particularly enjoyable, tearing themselves away from what is comfortable and well known can produce significant emotional responses.

5. **Acceptance:** Once the meaning of the changes is understood, and the new situation can be seen clearly, the emotions surrounding the change alter and take on a more positive tone. For most people, there comes a point when they accept that the change has taken place and that the past cannot be recreated. They then start thinking about the future and exploring the options available to them.

It was originally thought that these emotional states were sequential and that people experienced them in an orderly fashion. This is not always the case. As anyone knows who has been through a significant, traumatic change, the emotional reactions tend to be far more confused and random in their impact. Leaders have to be aware of the individual differences; for example, some members of the group might be able to insulate themselves from the pressures of change more effectively than others.

 COACH'S TIP

Never forget the 'people issues'

While developing a coherent strategy and deciding on an effective approach to change are essential components of the process of managing change, neglecting the people issues can be a recipe for disaster. As leaders of change, we need to be aware of this and be professional and sensitive when leading our people through change.

COACHING SESSION 61

The five psychological phases of change management

In the light of the five phases outlined above, write out what you feel would be the best approach that a leader could take at each stage.

Psychological phase	Possible leadership response
Denial	
Anger	
Bargaining	
Depression	
Acceptance	

Now have a look at the completed table below to see whether you identified all the leadership responses. Did you come up with any other ones?

Psychological phase	Possible leadership response
Denial	• Provide information as early as possible. • Provide information which is accurate and credible. • Explain the rationale for the change. • Offer face-to-face or counselling meetings (EAP). • Be prepared to repeat yourself.
Anger	• Let the person express themselves. • Listen to the person. • Recognize that the person is still in need of support (EAP). • Explain the rationale for the change or tactfully correct any inaccuracies.
Bargaining	• Listen and be prepared to recognize the employee's viewpoint. • Compromise if appropriate and if there is scope to do so. • Make concessions on the nature of the change to meet the needs of the individual if at all possible.
Depression	• Continue with the listening process. • Provide support and reassurance in the form of face-to-face meetings and counselling. • Remember that it's natural to feel sadness, regret, uncertainty, etc. It shows that the person has at least begun to accept the reality of the change.
Acceptance	• The employee is now ready to move on. • Follow a strategy of participation and involvement in the decision-making process. • Include the person in the planning and implementing of the change. • The emphasis here should be looking to the future – for example through training and development and perhaps even career opportunities.

→ NEXT STEPS

In this chapter we have looked at how managing change is a process with a set of defined stages, each of which need to be considered if the change is to be successful. We have seen that the development of a clear vision of the future sets the direction for a change initiative and facilitates the establishment of the change objectives. The use of effective analysis techniques enables organizations to identify the gaps that exist between their current position and their future visions. The identification of the change objectives and the long- and short-term goals allows resource needs to be identified and allows for measurement of the progress of the change initiative. We have also seen how leadership is a key role in the change process.

In the next chapter we will look at cross-cultural leadership. The world of business has no borders. Nationalization, globalization and the growth of multinational corporations introduce challenges that leaders must address. Effective cross-cultural leadership demands an understanding of the complexities of culture – from structural, political, social and psychological perspectives.

TAKEAWAYS

Why should we be concerned about managing change?

_____

_____

_____

_____

_____

_____

_____

_____

_____

_____

List the five psychological phases of change management.

1. _____

_____

2. _____

_____

3. _____

_____

4. _____

_____

5. _____

_____

What should a leader do to ensure that change is effectively implemented in an organization?

_____

_____

_____

_____

_____

_____

_____

_____

_____

_____

_____

_____

_____

_____

_____

_____

_____

_____

CROSS-CULTURAL LEADERSHIP

 OUTCOMES FROM THIS CHAPTER

- Think about the nature of culture and how to develop a definition of your own culture.
- Understand how we develop our personal cultural make-up.
- Learn about the six most prominent levels of culture.
- Discover how to improve cross-cultural communication.

'...culture and education aren't simply hobbies or minor influences.'

Pierre Bourdieu

Just what is culture? Culture is a complex concept, with many different definitions. Put simply, culture is about the way people think, feel and act. The famous cultural researcher Geert Hofstede has defined it as 'the collective programming of the mind distinguishing the members of one group or category of people from another'. This can refer to nations, regions, ethnicities, religions, occupations, organizations or genders. A simpler definition of culture is that it is 'the unwritten rules of the social game' (Hofstede 1980). The anthropologists Kevin Avruch and Peter Black (1993) define culture as something that 'provides the "lens" through which we view the world; the "logic" [...] by which we order it; the "grammar" [...] by which it makes sense'.

To be effective as leaders, we need to be aware of and take into account different cultures and the way they affect people's view of the world.

COACHING SESSION 62

Your culture

Without giving it a lot of thought, quickly write down how you would describe your culture in 25 words or fewer.

_____

_____

_____

_____

_____

_____

_____

_____

_____

_____

_____

_____

We obtain our initial cultural make-up during our first several years of life. In these important years we gain large amounts of cultural information, mostly from our parents but also from our wider family, from social groups and from our schooling. Civilizations and other groups develop culture over time. There are six main levels of culture:

- **National:** Today there are approximately 200 countries of all shapes and sizes. Research by Hofstede and others has demonstrated that these national cultures differ at the level of values, beliefs and behaviour. Examples of national cultures would be English, Kuwaiti, Canadian, etc.

■ **Regional:** Regional culture refers to the socio-political boundaries that exist in our world. Examples would be the notion of an 'African' culture (Africa is actually made up of 55 recognized nation states). In Finland, an example would be the difference between a person from Lapland and a person from Helsinki.

■ **Religious/ethnic:** Religious and ethnic boundaries have always existed. In today's world, they can be rather prominent. Consider here a Sunni Muslim and a Shia Muslim living in Bahrain, or a Roman Catholic and a Protestant in Northern Ireland.

■ **Organizational:** Most people spend a large part of their life in organizations of one type or another. This could be a corporation or employer body, a social club or an educational organization. Hofstede's research suggested that organizational cultures differ particularly in relation to what they do, and they can include symbols, rituals and heroes (Hofstede 1984). These are much easier to absorb than the first three levels of culture discussed above.

■ **Occupational:** Entering many occupations comes with a significant amount of mental programming. Consider medicine, engineering, psychotherapy, professional athletics, management or even 'working class'. Occupational cultures have symbols and rituals in common with organizational cultures, but they also often imply holding particular values and beliefs (e.g. medical ethics). It could be argued that a further level, 'class', is missing in this model, but in today's world class can be seen in the context of occupation.

■ **Gender:** It may look a bit odd to call gender a level of culture but it is useful to do so. In relation to all the previous five levels of culture, we can also have differences between men's culture and women's culture. The degree of gender differentiation is highly dependent on these other cultural levels. Hofstede suggests that this at least partially explains why it is hard to change traditional gender roles (1991).

COACHING SESSION 63

Levels of culture

Using the six levels of culture presented above, draw a map of your own cultural make-up. Fill in the diagram below with words that describe you for each of the levels of culture.

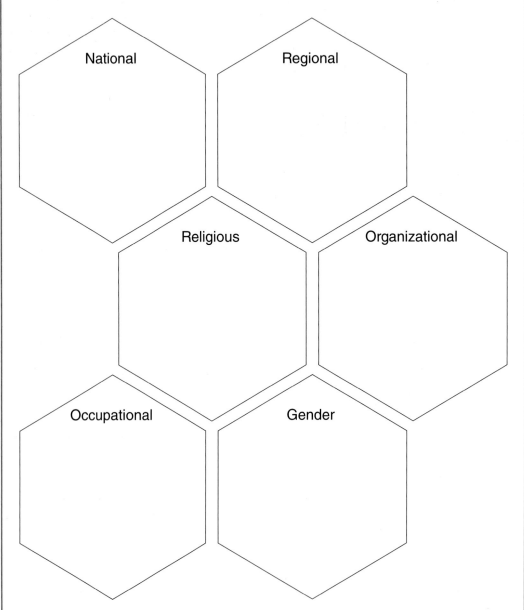

Was that difficult or easy to do? How does this visual map differ from the 25-word definition you wrote above?

CROSS-CULTURAL COMMUNICATION

As we saw in Chapter 4, anything that interferes with the transmission of a message is a barrier to communication.

Culture can be a significant barrier to effective communication. Of course, language can be a significant problem; it's hard to communicate if you speak only English and I speak only Chinese. But cross-cultural communication problems can also be about differences in how we see the world, how we process information, even how we view time. Avruch and Black (1993) suggest that when faced with a cultural interaction that we do not understand, we tend to interpret the others involved as 'weird' or 'wrong'.

COACHING SESSION 64

Cross-cultural communication problems

Have you ever been in a situation where you have experienced cross-cultural communication problems? Write down briefly what happened.

_____

_____

_____

_____

_____

_____

_____

_____

_____

_____

_____

_____

_____

CASE STUDY: HANK AND RAJESH

Rajesh is an expatriate from India working in Dubai. His fellow manager is another expatriate, Hank, who is from the United States. Rajesh believes that Hank comes across as loud and arrogant. Hank feels that Rajesh is too slow to act and comes across as condescending. Rajesh believes that he is a confident person and communicates well with others. Hank believes he is a confident person and communicates well with others. They have to work together on a new project and neither of them is looking forward to it.

COACHING SESSION 65

Case study: reflection

Answer these two questions arising from the Hank and Rajesh case study.

1. How likely is it that the two can develop a productive working relationship?

_____

_____

_____

_____

_____

_____

2. What do Rajesh and Hank need to do to improve their communication?

_____

_____

_____

_____

_____

_____

SIX STRATEGIES FOR EFFECTIVE CROSS-CULTURAL COMMUNICATION

To improve cross-cultural communication at any level, we need to learn and apply certain proven strategies. These are summarized in Figure 10.1 below.

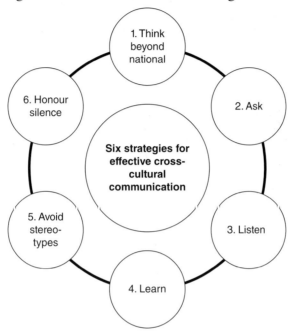

Figure 10.1 Six strategies for cross-cultural communication

1 Think beyond national

When communicating across cultures, we need to take into account that it is not just national culture that can be a problem. Just to look at national issues is to greatly limit our understanding of cross-cultural communication. Problems can also be at a regional, religious/ethnic, organizational, occupational and gender level. Have a look at the case study below – at what level do you think the problems are here?

CASE STUDY: MARY AND SIMON

Mary is an HR manager and she has been assigned to a project group under the direction of Simon, the most senior engineer in their oil services company. Neither of them is looking forward to working together on the project. Mary believes that Simon lacks people skills and that he has a problem working with strong women. Mary feels that all engineers are bad people managers and lack basic social skills. Simon believes that Mary is patronizing and doesn't understand the real work of the company. He thinks that all HR people are bossy and don't understand the real world or work. He calls HR the 'Business Prevention Unit'.

From this case study we can see organizational, occupational and gender cross-cultural issues. Both parties are stereotyping each other's occupational grouping. We can also see gender and even organizational stereotyping at play.

COACHING SESSION 66

Case study: reflection

As the leader of both Mary and Simon, how might you go about solving the cross-cultural problems between them? Consider the organizational, occupational and gender levels.

_____

_____

_____

_____

_____

_____

_____

_____

_____

_____

There are many possible strategies for you as the leader in this case. You could act as an informal mediator if you are familiar with all the cultures involved. You could serve as a 'translator' and explain the issues to both Mary and Simon. There is lots of talk in the modern workplace about 'diversity' and this case is an example of that. HR people and engineers need to understand how each other think and communicate and what that diversity adds to the organizational picture. If we learn how to better communicate with groups whose perspectives do not match our own, we can have a much better and stronger organization.

Simply put, diversity means difference. Recognizing diversity means understanding how people's differences and similarities can be used for the benefit of the individual and the organization. Mary and Simon need to understand that different people offer different skills, knowledge and attitudes that can improve the performance of the project team and even deliver a competitive advantage. If you look at the next examples, you will also see other strategies that the leader could apply in this case.

2 Ask

People are usually very happy to talk about their culture, be it national, regional or religious/ethnic. If you are wondering why someone does something that may appear unusual or strange to you, ask them. You can greatly increase your understanding simply by asking people questions about their cultures, customs and views.

COACH'S TIP

Be curious!

Most people enjoy being asked about their lives and their cultures and are happy when you show an interest in their culture. If you are generally interested and listen actively, you can learn a great deal about others and yourself.

For example, you might ask a Muslim why they fast during the period of Ramadan, or a Scotsman about wearing a kilt. It is wise to ask questions rather than jumping to conclusions and we may get answers that surprise us.

COACHING SESSION 67

Three questions

Have a go at answering the three questions below.

1. What number comes next in the sequence 1, 2, 3? _____
2. How many months are there in a year? _____
3. 'We eat food and we _____ water.'

If you are a person from the Western Hemisphere, you probably answered these three questions thus: '4', '12' and 'drink'. However, if you were an indigenous Australian from the Edward River Community in Far North Queensland, you would have answered these questions thus: 'many', 'very many' and 'eat'.

■ One, two, three, many... the local language, Kuuk Thaayorre, only goes to three and the word *mong* is best translated as 'many' because it can mean any number between 4 and 9.

- Those who say 12 (or 12.3682662 lunar months) are correct in European terms (solar) but irrelevant in Edward River terms. Apart from having no specific word to designate 12, *yurr mong*, or 'very many', is the right answer here. The annual cycle is understood in terms of environmental rhythms rather than in terms of fixed divisions of time.

- 'Eat' is the right word because, whereas we make a distinction between 'eating' and 'drinking', Kuuk Thaayorre does not and the locals use the same verb to describe both functions.

3 Listen

Do you remember the skills of active listening we discussed in Chapter 3? You may want to go back and review that section now.

When faced with cross-cultural communication, listening skills are essential. Reflecting back to the person what you have heard is one of the fundamental ways to improve cross-cultural communication. This is helpful because words and even gestures are frequently used differently between cultural groups. When there are language issues involved, it always makes sense to slow down, speak clearly and ensure that your pronunciation is intelligible.

4 Learn

Different cultures communicate differently. Cultural differences may be, for example, national (spoken language, writing, emotions), regional (accents, prejudices, taste) or occupational (class, jargon, attitude). As we just saw, asking questions and listening effectively are necessary skills to improve cross-cultural communication. But you can do more. You can actively learn about other cultures at all the six levels.

When it comes to humour, many cultures do not appreciate the use of humour and jokes in the business context. Many cultures have a certain etiquette when communicating and this can apply on all six levels. For example, with Mary and Simon in our case above, both parties have their own 'professional' ways of communicating.

One organization decided that it would run 'HR for non-HR training' so that non-HR staff (mainly operators and engineers) could develop a collaborative relationship with the HR department, rather than the antagonistic and competitive one that existed. By explaining how and why HR professionals thought, the non-HR professionals developed an understanding that started to bring down many of the barriers between departments. After the training, both groups had a more positive view of the other and some real results were seen in interdepartmental co-operation.

If you are going to work in a different cultural setting or with people from other cultures, it is important to get yourself educated about those cultures (on all six levels). This can be done through online research (but be careful about the reliability of the information) or through specialist training, coaching and mentoring.

🗣 COACHING SESSION 68

Global awareness quiz

How much do you know about other national cultures? Have a go at the global awareness quiz below.

Question	Your answer
What is the capital of Indonesia?	
Which country's flag is this? (The top half is red and the bottom white.)	
What is the most widely spoken language in the world?	

Question	Your answer
Which country has the largest number of English speakers?	
In a negotiation meeting in Tokyo you have waited in silence for Hanada-san's response to your offer. The silence becomes very uncomfortable and in frustration you offer a 20-per-cent reduction in price. Hanada-san closes his eyes and makes a deep sucking sound through his teeth. This is followed by more silence. What should you do next?	
In which country are the following cultural norms? • Attention should be paid to advance planning, promptness and punctuality. Businesspeople are informal yet direct. • Very soon after meeting, they do business on a first-name basis. Business cards are exchanged for information, without any special ceremony. • Luncheon meetings are common, but businesspeople do not usually schedule business during the evening or on weekends, which are dedicated to family and friends.	

You will find the correct answers to this quiz below.

Question	Answers
What is the capital of Indonesia?	The capital of Indonesia is Jakarta. Indonesia is an archipelago comprising approximately 17,508 islands. Indonesia has hundreds of different ethnic groups, each with unique cultural identities, and is influenced by Indian, Arabic, Chinese and European cultures.
Which country's flag is this? (The top half is red and the bottom white.)	This is the flag of Singapore. Officially the Republic of Singapore, it is a South-east Asian island city-state south of Malaysia. It is often named the most globalized country in the world and is a centre for international finance in the Asia-Pacific region.
What is the most widely spoken language in the world?	Mandarin Chinese is the first language of 12.44 per cent of the world's population, according to the *CIA World Factbook* (2012).
Which country has the largest number of English speakers?	India's English-speaking population has surpassed that of the United Kingdom and the United States. It is estimated that about a third of India's population of over a billion people speak conversational English.
In a negotiation meeting in Tokyo you have waited in silence for Hanada-san's response to your offer. The silence becomes very uncomfortable and in frustration you offer a 20-per-cent reduction in price. Hanada-san closes his eyes and makes a deep sucking sound through his teeth. This is followed by more silence. What should you do next?	Silence is important to Japanese people and is seen as a sign of respect. Sucking air through the teeth is a Japanese non-verbal sign of disapproval and frustration. Hanada-san is uncomfortable because you, by changing your price, seem unreliable. Additionally, remaining silent allows for reflection and the best response to this is further silence, not a different offer (Cook 2008).
In which country are the following cultural norms? • Attention should be paid to advance planning, promptness and punctuality. Businesspeople are informal yet direct. • Very soon after meeting, they do business on a first-name basis. Business cards are exchanged for information, without any special ceremony. • Luncheon meetings are common, but businesspeople do not usually schedule business during the evening or on weekends, which are dedicated to family and friends.	This is Australia. Australia is officially the Commonwealth of Australia. It is highly developed nation and one of the wealthiest. Since 1788, Australian culture has been strongly influenced by Anglo-Celtic Western culture. The indigenous Aboriginal and Torres Strait Islander cultures are complex and diverse and are the oldest living cultures in the world – they date back 50,000 to 65,000 years. Australia is a very multicultural country: over 20 per cent of Australians are foreign born and over 40 per cent are of mixed cultural origin.

ONLINE RESOURCE

You can download a template for this quiz by going to:

www.TYCoachbooks.com/Leadership

5 Avoid stereotypes

'[A stereotype is] a fixed, over-generalized belief about a particular group or class of people.'

Cardwell (1996)

The main advantages of stereotypes are that they simply save time. For example, 'I have dealt with Welsh people for years and I know that they generally prefer ...' Stereotyping allows us to simplify our complex world because it reduces how much thinking we have to do when we meet a new person.

A disadvantage of stereotypes is that they usually ignore important differences between people and we think things that are inaccurate (e.g. all engineers are ...). When we stereotype, we hear and see the things that we expected rather that what is real. We jump to incorrect assumptions.

Also, we usually see negative rather than positive images when stereotyping and so it should generally be avoided.

COACHING SESSION 69

Stereotypes

Are you a victim of stereotyping? Complete the questions below and see.

Statement	Opinion		
Real men don't cry.	☐ True	☐ False	☐ Possibly
You stop learning as you get older.	☐ True	☐ False	☐ Possibly
Russians never smile.	☐ True	☐ False	☐ Possibly
Drug addicts are all unemployed; they steal and hang around on street corners.	☐ True	☐ False	☐ Possibly

You have indicated your views on the stereotypes above. Let's see the facts.

Statement	Opinion	Fact
Real men don't cry.	False	In ancient Greece, 'men were expected to cry if their family's honour was at stake.' One of the greatest signs of true manliness was to shed tears. This idea was spread through most cultures, and continued through the Middle Ages and up to the Romantic period. Japanese samurai, medieval heroes and even Beowulf cried throughout their adventures. As recently as the nineteenth century, male tears were actually celebrated as a sign of honesty, integrity and strength (Sargent 1992). Psychologists will tell you that men who cry are emotionally stronger and healthier than those who don't.
You stop learning as you get older.	False	Like all parts of the body, the brain wears out and it used to be believed that it had no ability to repair itself. However, that is false. Researchers looking into myelination (the process by which a fatty layer accumulates around nerve cells) were surprised to discover that myelination isn't completed until young adulthood, not childhood as thought (Kluger 2013). *Time* reporter Jeffery Kluger reported that more recent studies '…have pushed the myelination limit even further. In some parts of the brain, including the temporal – which is involved with processing visual memories, language, meaning and emotions – insulating fat layers are still being laid down when we're in our 50s and even 60s' (Kluger 2013).
Russians never smile.	False	For Europeans, a smile is a simple expression of politeness. A smile, for most Russians, is something more intimate. Many Russians avoid smiling at strangers as they fear it can be easy misunderstood. According to Russian travel writer Varia Makagonova, 'It is a norm in Russia to have one's "serious face" on while in public places, […] showing too much emotion is considered strange and perhaps even impolite' (Makagonova 2013).
Drug addicts are all unemployed; they steal and hang around on street corners.	False	In fact, most drug users are in full-time employment (Buon 2007). Research by the International Labour Organization and the World Health Organization has suggested that 60 to 70 per cent of people with alcohol and other drug-related problems are in full-time employment (Buon 1990; ILO/WHO 1987).

We all stereotype and it would be unrealistic to totally exclude this from our life. Many people have grown up with prejudices passed on through their family, TV and the Internet. Unfortunately, these stereotypes can be harmful and limiting.

If you find yourself stereotyping, stop and ask yourself whether your opinions are based on experience, other people's views or fact. Become aware of the stereotypes you currently hold. If you catch yourself engaging in stereotypes, work to avoid discriminatory behaviour. Be flexible and be open to changing your views based on actual experience.

6 Honour silence

We saw above how, to a Japanese negotiator, silence is a positive response to an offer. But for an American it could indicate a lack of agreement. It is important to be aware of how silence is viewed by other cultures. Researcher Ikuko Nakane has pointed out that students in an Australian school who were relatively silent would be looked upon as having a problem, whereas the same behaviour in a Japanese school would be seen as a positive trait (2007).

You need to train yourself to be comfortable with silence, particularly when dealing with cultures that respect silence more than we do in the West. Speech communication expert Michael Kelly says: 'if there is nothing to comment on, don't talk or feel a need to talk. I observe many people talking, because they are nervous about being silent, or they feel they should say something. But often what they say is odd, or inane or redundant' (Kelly 2011). This is very sound advice. Silence does not always need to be filled; sometimes saying nothing is the best thing.

→ NEXT STEPS

In this chapter we have looked at culture. Culture is a complex concept, with many different definitions. Put simply, culture is about the way people feel, think and act. We acquire our cultural programming during childhood and we can view culture on six levels. We also saw how culture can be a significant filter to effective communication and how to minimize these problems using six strategies for effective cross-cultural communication: think beyond national, ask, listen, learn, avoid stereotypes and honour silence.

In the next chapter we will look at emotional intelligence (EI). We will look at the importance of this type of intelligence and explore whether it 'matters more than IQ'. We will also look at how you can improve your own emotional intelligence.

TAKEAWAYS

What do you think Hofstede means by his statement that culture is 'the collective programming of the mind'?

_____

_____

_____

_____

_____

_____

_____

What are the six levels of culture discussed in this chapter? Briefly define each.

1 _____

_____

2 _____

_____

3 _____

_____

4 _____

_____

5 _____

_____

6 _____

_____

How can you go about reducing the use of stereotyping in your communication with others?

_____

_____

_____

_____

_____

_____

_____

_____

EMOTIONAL INTELLIGENCE (EI)

✔ OUTCOMES FROM THIS CHAPTER

- Understand what emotional intelligence (EI) is and why it matters.
- Learn about the EI competence framework
- Know what the essential educational credentials are for a leader.
- Discover how to increase your own emotional intelligence (EI).

In his popular book *Emotional Intelligence: Why It Can Matter More Than IQ*, the psychologist Daniel Goleman brought the idea of EI to the general population. Goleman based his ideas on emerging work in neuroscience that showed that the emotional centres of the brain are involved in everything we think and do and are enormously important in our daily life. Goleman (1998) defines EI as:

> '...the capacity for recognising our own feelings and those of others, for motivating ourselves, and for managing emotions well in ourselves and in our relationships.'

Goleman did not 'invent' the idea of EI and we can trace the idea of emotional intelligence to the beginning of modern psychology. For instance, in 1937 E.L. Thorndike and his colleague S. Stein used the term 'social intelligence' to describe the skill of understanding, managing and getting along with other people. Wayne Payne, a doctoral student, is usually credited as the inventor of the term 'emotional intelligence', which he used in his 1985 doctoral dissertation on emotion.

COACHING SESSION 70

EI: your present knowledge

What do you already know about EI? Have you read anything on the subject? What do you think would be the main components of EI?

_____

_____

_____

_____

_____

_____

_____

AN EI FRAMEWORK

IQ (intelligence quotient) is a score derived from a standardized test designed to assess intelligence. IQ scores are a good predictor of educational achievement, but Goleman suggests they take second place to EI in determining outstanding job performance (Goleman 1998). Goleman suggests that there are five measurements of EI, each with corresponding competencies. These can be summarized as follows:

Measurement	Example
Self-awareness	_Understanding your own internal states, strengths and weaknesses._ Self-confidence and accurate self-assessment are essential components.
Self-regulation	_Managing your emotions and impulses._ Self-control and taking responsibility for yourself are part of this, as are adaptability and innovation.
Motivation	The need to achieve. The inner drive to improve yourself. Commitment, optimism and initiative. Goal-setting would also be part of this.
Empathy	_Putting yourself into another person's shoes._ Understanding and wanting to help others develop. This includes service orientation and political awareness.
Social skills	_Communication skills._ Conflict management, influence and leadership are significant here, as are teamwork and being a change leader.

CRITICISMS OF EI

Goleman's theories have been very influential, particularly in the business sector and with corporate trainers. However, there are critics of his work. Some researchers have given EI the 'pop psychology' label (Mayer, Roberts & Barsade 2008). Other critics have questioned the validity and reliability of Goleman's research. However, most critics agree that the concept of EI is valid but suggest that more empirical research is needed to give complete scientific weight to the theories.

COACHING SESSION 71

EI competences

Using the above EI competence framework, can you come up with an example of each from your own work as a leader?

Measurement	Example from your work as a leader
Self-awareness	
Self-regulation	
Motivation	
Empathy	
Social skills	

Measurement one above is 'self-awareness'. This is all about recognizing your own emotions and their effects. The first step in understanding emotions is to accurately distinguish them. The next coaching session will help you do that.

COACHING SESSION 72

Understanding your emotions

Think of an intense emotional reaction (e.g. anger, confusion, frustration) you have had recently in your team or with a team member and write it down in the box:

Score the emotion using the following scale:

1————+————+————+————5————+————+————+————+————10

Low   Average   Overwhelming

What was the situation (e.g. colleague not doing something, some else taking credit for my work, etc.) that caused the intense feeling?

_____

_____

Why did it matter to you?

_____

_____

What personal value and/or principle was involved?

_____

_____

What have you discovered about your emotions from this coaching session?

_____

_____

_____

_____

_____

_____

Self-awareness provides the underlying basis for effective leadership. Developing self-awareness requires an understanding of your true feelings. If you learn to evaluate your emotions, you can learn to manage them. This is vital for the effective leader.

EDUCATIONAL CREDENTIALS AND CREDENTIALISM

If EI is more important than intelligence, what does this tell us about employers who insist on higher and higher credentials for employment? What is the true value of educational credentials?

Credentials were first used in the nineteenth century, their main purpose being to protect the public by showing the competence of the professional. Over the past hundred years there has been great growth in the number of people who have credentials, a growth in the number of credential-granting bodies and a growth in the use of credentials as a way of selecting people for employment. Credentials are used for employee selection mainly because of their administrative convenience and the illusion of equity that they convey (Watts 1985).

'Credentialism' is the empty pursuit of degrees or other credentials that are not necessarily related to intellectual or educational achievement (Arnsteein 1982). Credentialism occurs when entry qualifications for an occupation are upgraded but there is no commensurate change in the knowledge or skill requirements for the job.

Credentialism can be lessened if certification accurately reflects actual skill competencies. In relation to recruitment, where the process is aimed at predicting future success, it makes no sense to rely on only one indicator such as educational credentials. Most employers view experience as a better indication of potential work performance than educational credentials (Buon & Compton 1990).

It appears that in demanding credentials for particular occupations, employers' reasons fall into two rather crude categories:

1. **The investment effect:** Credentials show that the applicant has undergone certain educational training that has made them more productive.

2. **The screening effect:** Education, and hence credentials, show particular attributes in the applicant that the employer wants.

This is an uneasy dichotomy and it is probable that in every case the screening and the investment effect would coexist (Buon 1994).

Rather than assume a direct correlation between educational credentials and future job success, a more useful approach is to analyse fully the job(s) in question. This is a method of systematically compiling, maintaining, reviewing and modifying information about the job and the person to fill it. Where educational credentials are required for a specific position, the employer bears the responsibility for proving that those educational credentials are necessary for the effective performance of that job. If the employer cannot do this, then credentials should not be specified.

This is not to suggest that education has no value, for it clearly does. In many cases, particularly in the professions, job analysis may indicate the need for credentials in order that the incumbent be able to practise (medicine, law). In other cases, the detailed knowledge required to perform a particular job may be available only from a course at the tertiary level (pharmacy, teaching). And while those with higher educational credentials do appear to have higher personal incomes, it is important to note that educational credentials are not sources of income in their own right.

COACHING SESSION 73

Guess who?

When you look at the following list of well-known people, can you guess which of them did not have formal university credentials?

Name	Does he/she have formal university credentials?		
Simon Cowell – music executive and TV mogul	Yes	No	Don't know
John Glenn – astronaut and US Senator	Yes	No	Don't know
Richard Branson – founder of Virgin and entrepreneur	Yes	No	Don't know
Srinivasa Ramanujan – famous mathematician	Yes	No	Don't know
Henry Ford – industrialist and entrepreneur	Yes	No	Don't know
Doris Lessing – Nobel Prize in Literature laureate	Yes	No	Don't know
Bill Gates – Microsoft billionaire and philanthropist	Yes	No	Don't know
Mary Kay Ash – cosmetics mogul and entrepreneur	Yes	No	Don't know
Michael Dell – founder of Dell Computers	Yes	No	Don't know
Claude Monet – painter	Yes	No	Don't know
Walt Disney – founder of the Walt Disney Company	Yes	No	Don't know
John D. Rockefeller – billionaire and philanthropist	Yes	No	Don't know
Coco Chanel – founder of fashion brand Chanel	Yes	No	Don't know
Wolfgang Puck – famous chef and entrepreneur	Yes	No	Don't know

The correct answer is none of them. All of these highly influential and successful people did not have formal university credentials (though many of them have received honorary degrees). This is not to imply that credentials have no value – they clearly do. However, Goleman reports that in the modern world of business – on the basis of analysis conducted by dozens of different experts in almost 500 organizations – EI has a paramount place in excellence on the job – virtually *any* job.

WORKING ON YOUR EI

According to Goleman, unlike IQ (which remains stable throughout life), EI continues to be learned and increases over every decade of life (1998). The evidence that people can improve on their EI competencies comes from multiple sources (Boyatzis, Cowan & Kolb 1995). The simple fact is that you can learn to get better at EI.

COACHING SESSION 74

EI: accurate self-assessment

One of the key ways to increase your emotional intelligence is by accurate self-assessment. Getting feedback from a variety of sources is a great way of developing a well-balanced and accurate understanding of you – *as you really are*.

In this coaching session, you need to approach someone you trust and get feedback from them on your behaviour as a leader. Ask someone to meet with you for about 30 minutes. Go to a private place where you won't be disturbed and get their feedback on the following areas. If you really want extra impact, copy the sheet and get feedback from more than one person.

Ask each person the following questions:

1. How would you describe my communication skills?

   _____

   _____

   _____

   _____

2. How do I perform as a leader?

   _____

   _____

   _____

   _____

3. What is the one thing that I do as a leader that annoys or frustrates you?

_____

_____

_____

_____

4. Can you remember the last time I gave you positive feedback? What did I do well or what could I have improved in this case?

_____

_____

_____

_____

5. How would you rate me on my ability to demonstrate empathy?

_____

_____

_____

_____

6. What could I do to become a better leader?

_____

_____

_____

_____

Take this feedback and incorporate it into the picture you have of yourself. What did you learn? What could you improve? This process of self-examination and reflection is boosting your EI as you do it.

ONLINE RESOURCE

You can download a template for this EI interview by going to:

www.TYCoachbooks.com/Leadership

Here are some other ways to improve your EI:

- Think about how you last responded in a conflict situation. How did this conflict develop – was it resolved? How?

- Demonstrate genuine humility.

- Observe what causes you stress.

- Examine how you respond to stressful situations.

- Motivate yourself to make the changes.

- Observe how you react to people who disagree with you.

- Examine how you handle disappointments.

- Is there something that other people do that that triggers an emotion in you? Do you know the source of these triggers?

- What makes you really upset in meetings?

- Can you always keep your emotions under control when things go wrong? If not, what stops you being in control?

- Take time to write things down – journaling can really increase your EI.

- Take responsibility for your actions.

- Examine how your actions will affect others.

- Look for role models and copy their way of doing things.

- What causes you to experience 'road-rage'?

- What do you like about yourself? Make a list.

- Get feedback from other people.

COACHING SESSION 75

Improving your EI competency

Choose three of the items from the list of ways to improve your EI above. Write them down below and decide what action you will take to implement them in your life.

1. _____

2. _____

3. _____

NEXT STEPS

In this chapter we have looked at emotional intelligence (EI) and seen that it is the ability to observe, distinguish, control and appraise our emotions. The aim is to use our awareness of EI to manage our behaviour and relationships. Daniel Goleman suggests that there are five measurements of EI: self-awareness, self-regulation, motivation, empathy and social skills. While our present understanding of EI is good, there is still a vast amount to be discovered.

In the next chapter we will look at problem solving and decision making. We will explore some practical tools to improve your decision-making and problem-solving ability. These are key skills for any leader.

TAKEAWAYS

How would you describe emotional intelligence (EI) in 25 words or fewer?

_____

_____

_____

_____

_____

_____

_____

_____

_____

Why do some employers rely heavily on educational credentials as a way to select people for employment? Do you agree with this?

_____

_____

_____

_____

_____

_____

_____

_____

_____

Would you rather have a better IQ or a better EI? Why?

_____

_____

_____

_____

_____

_____

_____

_____

_____

_____

LEADERSHIP DECISION MAKING

 OUTCOMES FROM THIS CHAPTER

- Understand what leadership decision making is and why it is important.

- Learn how to use appropriate leadership decision-making techniques.

- Discover how to use practical tools such as brainstorming, the Crawford Slip Method and PMI.

- Know what 'groupthink' is and how to recognize and avoid it when making decisions.

Decision making seems natural; it should, because we make decisions constantly. Most of our decision making is unconscious – that is, we don't give it much thought. But as leaders we are responsible for making judgements and choosing between alternatives that may have a tremendous impact on many people and our organizations. Most of our leadership decisions are made rapidly and without the assistance of formal 'decision-making tools'. This is understandable, because you simply wouldn't have enough time to do anything else.

Simple decisions need only a simple decision-making process. But difficult decisions may require more complex and formal methods. When we have to make a difficult decision, we need to take into account various factors:

- **Complexity:** Deciding what 'shirt to wear today' is usually straightforward, but some choices are so dense and involved that deciding between the different factors requires a more formal process.

- **Risk:** Risk implies that we have a choice to influence the outcome of a decision. But risk involves consequences and can also make the result of a decision costly and stifle our rational decision-making processes.

- **People:** Interpersonal issues add a layer of complexity that makes decisions difficult. People do not always act rationally or consistently, and this means that making decisions involving people can be really hard.

Decision making is an essential leadership skill. If you develop your skills in this area, you can become a better and more successful leader.

COACHING SESSION 76

Leadership decisions you make

What sort of decisions do you need to make as a leader? Consider the last three significant decisions you made as a leader and then complete the table below.

Decision	Factors involved	What happened?
1	Complexity	
	Risk	
	People	
2	Complexity	
	Risk	
	People	
3	Complexity	
	Risk	
	People	

When you look at your examples of decision making, what did you learn about how you make decisions? What did you do well? What could you have done better? Are there particular types of decision that you find difficult to make?

_____

_____

_____

_____

_____

_____

_____

_____

_____

_____

_____

Effective decision making requires a systematic approach so that you can make decisions with confidence and demonstrate good leadership. So, how good are you at making decisions? Complete this short quiz to help you evaluate your decision-making skills.

THE LEADERSHIP DECISION-MAKING PROCESS

A systematic decision-making process helps you address the necessary components that result in a good decision. By taking an ordered approach, you're less likely to miss things or get caught up in interpersonal or political issues and you will make better-quality decisions.

 ONLINE RESOURCE

You can download a template for the following quiz by going to:

www.TYCoachbooks.com/Leadership

💬💬 COACHING SESSION 77

Decision-making quiz

Complete the following quiz being as honest as you can. Remember to answer questions according to how you really are – not how you wish to be.

Question	Never	Rarely	Often	Always
I use a formal process in decision making.	1	2	3	4
I rely on my 'gut instincts' when making decisions.	4	3	2	1
I take time to choose a tool for each specific decision.	1	2	3	4
There is a formal structure to my decision making.	1	2	3	4
I 'toss a coin' or use random decision-making processes.	4	3	2	1
I find it easy to generate possible solutions.	1	2	3	4
It is a good idea to involve others in decision making.	1	2	3	4
I am aware of and try to avoid 'groupthink'.	1	2	3	4
I rely on my own experience to find potential solutions.	4	3	2	1
After a decision is made I review and evaluate the process.	1	2	3	4
Subtotal				
Grand total				

Score interpretation

Score	Comment
10–21	You need to improve your decision-making skills. You need to be more systematic and objective in your decision making. Read this chapter carefully for advice on how to develop a decision-making process. A good first step will be to learn and use some of the practical tools discussed below. With more practice, and by following a more structured approach, you'll be able to develop this skill and start solving problems more efficiently.
22–31	You have reasonable decision-making skills, but they could improve. Review your scores above to see where you lost points and work on these areas. Try using some of the decision-making tools explored in this chapter. You understand the process but don't always follow it. By committing yourself to a decision-making process, you'll see significant improvements
32–40	You make decisions efficiently – well done! Keep looking for new ways to further improve your practice. Try using some of the tools covered in this chapter that you haven't tried before. Make sure that you continue to perfect your skills and use them for continuous improvement as a leader.

There are five steps to making an effective decision (see Figure 12.1):

1. Decide how to decide
2. Generate possible solutions
3. Evaluate possible solutions
4. Make choices
5. Implement and evaluate choices

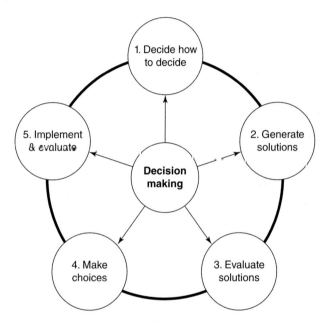

Figure 12.1 A systematic leadership decision-making process

1 DECIDE HOW TO DECIDE

If you are going to make an effective decision, then you must assess the best way to make that decision. The Vroom–Yetton Model was developed by Victor Vroom and Phillip Yetton in the 1970s and assists in the selection of the best leadership style for group decision making. This model provides a structure for deciding how to decide.

This model identifies five different styles of decision making based both on the situation and level of involvement indicated. They are:

Leadership style	Description
Autocratic type 1 (A1)	The leader makes the decision using the information available and uses an autocratic style of leadership.
Autocratic type 2 (A2)	The leader collects information from others and then makes the decision. The final decision may or may not be shared with the group.

Leadership style	Description
Consultative Type 1 (C1)	Using a consultative leadership style, the leader consults with people to get their opinions. The leader will then make the decision.
Consultative Type 2 (C2)	Again using a consultative leadership style, the leader consults the group to get their opinions and suggestions. The leader will then make the decision.
Group (G)	Using a collaborative leadership style, the group will make the decision using consensus. The leader plays a supportive role. This is linked to the transformative leadership style (see Chapter 1).

So how do you determine which decision-making style to use? Vroom & Yetton provide a set of questions so that leaders can choose which of the five styles to use (Vroom & Yetton 1973; Vroom & Jago 1988). The following eight questions need to be followed in sequence:

1. **Quality Requirement (QR):** How important is the technical quality of the decision?

2. **Commitment Requirement (CR):** How important is subordinate commitment to the decision?

3. **Leader's Information (LI):** Do you (the leader) have enough information to make a high-quality decision by yourself?

4. **Problem Structure (ST):** Is the problem well structured (e.g. defined, clear, organized, lends itself to a solution, time limited)?

5. **Commitment Probability (CP):** If you were to make the decision by yourself, is it reasonably certain that your subordinates would be committed to a decision?

6. **Goal Congruence (GC):** Do subordinates share the organizational goals to be attained in solving the problem?

7. **Subordinate Conflict (CO):** Is conflict among subordinates over the preferred solutions expected?

8. **Subordinate Information (SI):** Do subordinates have sufficient information to make a high-quality decision?

Using the answers to these eight questions, we can find out which decision-making leadership style is best, from the following graph (Figure 12.2).

The model is highly flexible with respect to the choices a leader can make in decision making. However, there may be times where you would not use the model. This would include emergency situations or where there is an extremely large group involved in the decision.

In 1988 Vroom replaced the 'decision tree' system with a system based on mathematics. You will see this described as the Vroom–Yetton–Jago Model. We have not gone into this more mathematical model here, but you can read about it on various online sites, if you are interested.

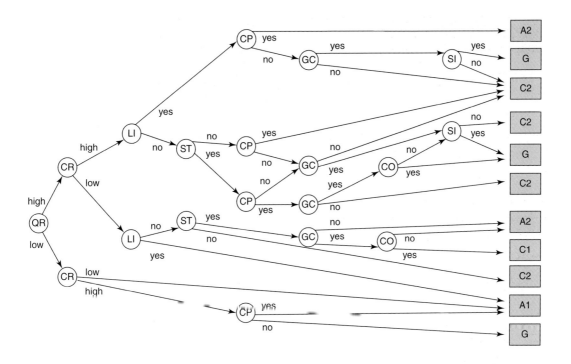

Figure 12.2 'Decision tree' (based on Vroom & Yetton 1973 and Vroom & Jago 1988)

Other tools

There are other tools available to help you make decisions about how to make decisions, but we will not be exploring them in this workbook. Examples include Stakeholder Analysis and the Five Whys Method. There are also many helpful tools to help you identify the cause(s) of a problem. These include Root Cause Analysis (RCA) and Cause-and-Effect Analysis.

COACHING SESSION 78

Leadership decision-making graph

Use one of the three decisions you wrote down in Coaching session 76 above and follow the decision tree to see what the Vroom–Yetton Decision Model would suggest was the best leadership style to use. Did you get this right? What style did you use? Do you agree with the suggestion made by the model?

2 GENERATE POSSIBLE SOLUTIONS

This is a critical step in making good decisions. Generally speaking, the more options and possible solutions you can generate, the more effective you will be. Some of the common tools include brainstorming, mind-mapping, reframing, affinity diagrams and the Crawford Slip Method. In this workbook we are going to look at two of these tools – brainstorming and the Crawford Slip Method.

Brainstorming

> *'It is easier to tone down a wild idea than to think up a new one.'*
>
> Alex F. Osborn, 1963

Most people have been involved in a 'brainstorm' at some time and the term is often used to refer to any type of group discussion. However, you have also probably found that brainstorms don't work very well. This is because people usually do not know how to run one correctly.

The term and the method first appeared in 1942, in a book called *How to Think Up* by Alex F. Osborn, an American advertising executive (Osborn 1942). The strategy was to be totally uninhibited and unrestricted in generating ideas. Since Osborn's work, psychological researchers have come up with many ways to improve on his ideas. Brainstorming works best with about a half-dozen people, but it can work with up to 20 people or with only three.

The **steps for brainstorming** are as follows:

1. The person facilitating the brainstorm reviews the problem or question, so that everyone fully understands it.

2. Then the problem is written on a whiteboard or flipchart.

3. The participants take five minutes to think quietly about the problem and to come up with a 'bank' of ideas. People can write at this stage but not speak. With a large group, the leader should enlist the help of a 'scribe' to record the comments on a screen or flipchart.

4. The leader now invites people to suggest ideas, usually within a set time limit. Here there are two methods that can be used: round-robin or popcorn. The decision about which method to use should be based on the leader's knowledge of the group.

   ■ *Round-robin:* Here participants take turns contributing an idea, going around the group one by one (passing if they have nothing to say) until everyone has exhausted their bank of ideas or any ideas they have 'piggybacked' on others' ideas. Round-robin is a better for people who are less aggressive and more methodical. It also suits certain national cultures (those that are less vocal and assertive).

- *Popcorn:* This is the method often used by inexperienced leaders and it doesn't always work well. Here participants shout out their ideas in any order, until they have nothing left to say. With the popcorn method, it may be harder for quiet people to participate; people can also become very excitable and hard for the leader to control. Again, this method works better with particular groups.

Depending on the group, you may want to set a time limit for the brainstorm. Some groups seem to work better with a deadline and you may have to practise this with a group to see what works best. If you decide to set a time limit but the ideas are still coming as the allotted finishing time approaches, don't hesitate to extend the time.

The **rules for a brainstorming session** should be as follows:

- Create a comfortable environment.

- Let participants know that they are totally free to offer any ideas.

- Record all ideas, leaving nothing out.

- Keep a fast-moving pace for the brainstorming section.

- Don't react to any ideas – there should be no criticisms or other judgements (verbal or non-verbal).

- All comments should be made to the group; no side discussions are allowed.

- One person speaks at a time, with no interruption.

- Build on ideas (hitchhike or piggyback) – add, shift, combine.

- Don't get caught up in details or differences.

If the brainstorming session has generated too many good ideas, then you may want to consider using the KJ Method. This is named after its developer, the Japanese anthropologist Kawakita Jiro. This method is also called an affinity diagram. This helps to combine large amounts of data by finding relationships between ideas.

The steps for the KJ (affinity diagram) Method are as follows:

1. Take the brainstormed list and put it on cards or sticky notes.

2. Look for ideas that seem to be linked.

3. Move ideas into 'affinity' sets, creating groups of related ideas.

4. Once sorted into groups, sort large clusters into subgroups for easier management and analysis.

5. When a majority of the ideas have been sorted, add titles for each affinity set.

While group brainstorming is usually very effective at generating ideas, several studies have shown that individual brainstorming usually produces more ideas. It appears that the concentration and insight required for us to generate new ideas are often inhibited by the presence of others.

COACHING SESSION 79

Personal brainstorm

Take one of the three decisions you wrote down in Coaching session 76 and try to do a personal brainstorm to come up with possible solutions. Use the rules for brainstorming where they usefully apply to individual brainstorming. Remember that quantity, not quality, is important at this stage.

The Crawford Slip Method

This technique was developed by Dr C.C. Crawford, an educationalist, in the 1920s. The process involves collecting on slips of paper a large number of ideas from a group. As with brainstorming, the leader displays a problem, then participants write out possible solutions on the provided slips of paper (nowadays people often use sticky notes). According to Crawford, because this is an anonymous process, more open and creative ideas result. It is a bit like brainstorming but on slips of paper.

The steps for the Crawford Slip Method are as follows:

1. Distribute to each person paper slips, index cards or sticky notes – depending on the problem, between 5 and 25 slips each.

2. Describe the problem to be solved and, to get people thinking, tell people how their ideas will be used.

3. Let them know that everyone is expected to contribute ideas and also help with the task of sorting.

4. Ask people to write down as many suggestions as they can – one idea per slip.

5. Encourage people to keep contributing until they run out – when most people have stopped writing, it's time to end the session, but do allow at least 15 to 20 minutes.

6. Sort the contributions into logical groupings and similar ideas by posting them on a wall or board (you could use the more formal affinity diagram technique at this step instead).

7. Reduce the entire list initially produced on paper slips to anywhere between three and ten broad headings (you can also use subgroups).

8. As the sorting process proceeds, get people to sort and resort. Consensus on the categorization is the goal.

9. Record the number of slips containing each suggestion.

The Crawford Slip Method works extremely well and helps people get involved, but it can produce a lot of frustration at the sorting step. Leaders and facilitators should be prepared to deal with problems as they arise. This tool can generate a wide variety of solutions to potential problems.

COACHING SESSION 80

Use the Crawford Slip Method

For this coaching session you will need to go beyond the workbook. Using a group of people you know well, use the steps above and try to use the Crawford Slip Method to generate ideas about one of the three decisions you wrote down in Coaching session 76. Use the steps above. Then come back to the workbook and record how it went.

3 EVALUATE POSSIBLE SOLUTIONS

This step requires the leader to state, as clearly as possible, all the decision alternatives available. For example, if you are deciding which new smartphone to buy, think about whether the decision options consist only of the different types of smartphone, whether it is about operating systems (Android, etc.) or whether another option might be to keep the phone you have.

When you're satisfied that you have a good selection of realistic alternatives, you need to assess the practicality, risks and implications of each option. Some of the most popular and effective analytical tools include: Cost–Benefit Analysis, Six Thinking Hats, Risk Analysis, Force Field Analysis, and the Plus, Minus, Interesting (PMI) technique. We will look in detail at PMI here.

The PMI tool

PMI is a simple but useful tool for making decisions. It's used to weigh the pros and cons of alternatives, particularly actions. This method was developed by lateral thinking guru Edward de Bono and discussed in his 1982 book *De Bono's Thinking Course.*

The steps for PMI are as follows:

1. On the flipchart or whiteboard the leader or facilitator draws three columns, headed 'Plus', 'Minus' and 'Interesting'.

2. Write down the action under consideration.

3. In the 'Plus' column list all of the positive points for taking the action.

4. In the 'Minus' column list all of the negative points against taking the action.

5. In the 'Interesting' column list all of the 'interesting' implications of taking the action.

6. At this stage, it may be obvious what you should do. If not, assign a positive or negative score to each point. Add up the scores. A positive score indicates support for an action, while a negative score suggests that you should avoid this action.

If you only want to decide whether to take one particular action or not, you need only perform the PMI process once. However, if you have several options, you will need to consider each decision individually, and then weigh the results against each other. It is also important to remember to 'sense-check' your scores, particularly if your scoring system is quite subjective.

Here is an example of a PMI for choosing a particular model of smartphone:

+ Plus +	– Minus –	? Interesting?
Purchasing an Android smartphone		
Lots of apps	Lots of viruses	Google supports it
My friends all have it	Poor battery life	Most popular system
Lots of phone choices	Not as simple as iOS	Open source
Cheaper than an iPhone	It's not an iPhone	Windows Phone 8
Multitasking	I'm used to my Blackberry	
Cool and trendy		

If the decision is still not clear, you could score each of the columns – though, in this example, as you are a cool and trendy person, you have already decided on an Android.

COACHING SESSION 81

PMI

Insert your own action or alternative in the table below where indicated.

1. In the 'Plus' column list all of the positive points for taking the action.
2. In the 'Minus' column list all of the negative points against taking the action.
3. In the 'Interesting' column list all of the 'interesting' implications of taking the action.

If the issue under consideration is a series of alternatives, you would do a PMI for both or all of the alternatives, following the procedure described above (make copies of this sheet).

+ Plus +	– Minus –	? Interesting?
Your action:		

ONLINE RESOURCE

You can download a template for this PMI template by going to:

www.TYCoachbooks.com/Management

4 MAKE CHOICES

When you have evaluated all your choices, the decision may be obvious. However, if the choice of the best alternative is still not clear, you may need to use other tools such as Grid-Analysis, Nominal Group Technique or the Delphi Method.

5 IMPLEMENT AND EVALUATE CHOICES

After the information has been considered, a decision based on that information should be made and implemented. Also, because not all the decisions are likely to be good ones, the final step in this five-step decision-making process is to evaluate whether your decision was determined and implemented correctly. Take time to reflect on your decision-making process and you will improve your leadership skills in this area. In particular, you need to check that **groupthink** has not contaminated the decision-making process.

Groupthink refers to the tendency for group members to strive to agree with one another, with the result that this interferes with rational, constructive decision-making processes (Janis 1983). Groups that become contaminated by groupthink fail to analyse critically and discuss adequately alternative courses of action. This results in defective decision making.

The social psychologist Irving Janis first identified this phenomenon in the 1970s through his study of US government policy-making groups (Janis 1972). Two disastrous incidents – the decision to invade Cuba at the Bay of Pigs in 1961 and the failure to protect Pearl Harbor against Japanese attack in 1941 – were attributed to groupthink. In recent times, the Space Shuttle *Challenger* disaster and the decision to invade Iraq for 'weapons of mass destruction' have also been attributed to groupthink.

Some of the classic symptoms of groupthink are:

- direct pressure put on anyone who doesn't go along with the group's decision
- disregard of concerns that deviate from the group consensus
- stereotyped and negative views of anyone opposed to the group's decision
- an avoidance of conflict
- an unquestioned belief in the group's ethics
- over-confidence in the group's abilities
- lack of consideration of alternative views
- an illusion of unanimity
- the downplaying of any warnings that the wrong decision has been made
- no proper risk analysis or other formal decision-making processes
- selection bias in obtaining information
- self-censorship – people keep any objections to themselves.

Groupthink can be apparent in any organizational situation where groups are required to make important decisions. It is a particular tendency in highly cohesive groups which have been successful in the past and in groups with particularly dominant leaders. However, if you are aware of groupthink, several relatively simple steps can be taken to minimize the problem. Janis (1983) suggests the following:

- Choose an impartial group leader.
- Strongly encourage each group member to raise their doubts or objections.
- Use 'experts' to raise questions and doubts.
- Use 'second chance' meetings so that previously decided decisions can be overturned.

COACHING SESSION 82

Groupthink

Using the table below, consider a poor decision you are familiar with (either from history or your own organization) and examine it below for groupthink.

Symptom	Present?		
Direct pressure put on anyone who doesn't go along with the group's decision (look for this inside and outside the group)	Yes ☐	No ☐	Possibly ☐
Group members disregard concerns that deviate from the group consensus (people screen what they don't want to hear or see)	Yes ☐	No ☐	Possibly ☐
Stereotyped and negative views of anyone opposed to the group's decision (sometimes done in a 'joking' way)	Yes ☐	No ☐	Possibly ☐
An avoidance of conflict (see Chapter 7)	Yes ☐	No ☐	Possibly ☐
An unquestioned belief in the group's ethics (see Chapter 12)	Yes ☐	No ☐	Possibly ☐
Over-confidence in the group's abilities (the group sees itself as invincible and infallible)	Yes ☐	No ☐	Possibly ☐
No consideration of alternative views (use of mindguards; alternatives downplayed)	Yes ☐	No ☐	Possibly ☐
Illusion of unanimity (you are with us or against us)	Yes ☐	No ☐	Possibly ☐
The downplaying of any warnings that the wrong decision has been made	Yes ☐	No ☐	Possibly ☐
No proper risk analysis or other formal decision-making processes (hidden risks and alternatives not evaluated)	Yes ☐	No ☐	Possibly ☐
Selection bias in obtaining information	Yes ☐	No ☐	Possibly ☐
Self-censorship – people keep any objections to themselves	Yes ☐	No ☐	Possibly ☐

→ NEXT STEPS

In this chapter we looked at how simple decisions need only a simple decision-making process. But difficult decisions may require more complex and formal processes. We have seen how an organized and systematic decision-making process usually leads to better-quality decisions. We also learned about the five steps to making an effective decision. Finally, we looked at the dangers of groupthink.

The next chapter is the final chapter. Here we will summarize the many necessary skills and competencies of a great leader that we have covered in this workbook. We will consider how you can become your own leadership coach – that is, how you can take full control of your own development towards becoming a great leader.

TAKEAWAYS

There are five steps to making an effective decision. List them below:

1

_____

_____

2

_____

_____

3

_____

_____

4

_____

_____

5

_____

_____

An organized and systematic decision-making process usually leads to better-quality decisions. In what practical ways can you improve decision making in your leadership role?

_____

_____

_____

_____

_____

_____

_____

_____

_____

_____

_____

_____

How would you go about reducing the risk of groupthink in your organization? Try to list at least five to six practical steps.

1 _____

_____

2 _____

_____

3 _____

_____

4 _____

_____

5 _____

_____

6 _____

BECOMING YOUR OWN LEADERSHIP COACH

13

✔ OUTCOMES FROM THIS CHAPTER

- Learn how to apply all you have learned in this workbook to becoming your own leadership coach.

> *'The test of a good coach is that, when they leave, others will carry on successfully.'*

> Anon.

Throughout this workbook, we have covered many of the necessary skills and competencies of a great leader. We have looked at communication skills, delegation, strategy, change management, motivation and decision making. We have looked at how you can improve your time management, team leadership and cross-cultural capabilities. We have also looked at how you can develop your emotional intelligence (EI). Effectively, you have been 'coached': you have gone through a process that is used for guiding and supporting a person as they learn something new and develop their abilities.

Moving on from this workbook, you should consider how you can become your own leadership coach – that is, how to take full control of your own development towards becoming a great leader. Self-leadership is crucial in this process, as is self-awareness and self-motivation.

 ## COACHING SESSION 83

Are you ready?

Are you ready to become your own leadership coach? Take the following quiz to see.

See whether you have the qualities to be your own coach. Here are various statements related to coaching yourself. Read the statement and indicate whether you 'agree' or 'disagree'. Be as honest as you can when answering – remember that your answers should relate to how you presently are, not how you want to be.

STATEMENT	Agree ☑	Disagree ☑
I realize that I need to change things about myself.	☐	☐
I believe I have more to learn about leadership.	☐	☐
Improving my communication skills is an ongoing task.	☐	☐
Receiving feedback is valuable to me.	☐	☐
I believe that I have more to learn about myself.	☐	☐
I value feedback on my behaviour and actions.	☐	☐
I try to keep up to date with new developments in my area.	☐	☐
I am willing to change how I do things, if necessary.	☐	☐
I am open to new ideas about people management.	☐	☐
Flexibility in leadership is valuable to me.	☐	☐
I want to improve my emotional intelligence.	☐	☐
I want to understand more fully why I believe certain things.	☐	☐
I set and work towards SMART goals.	☐	☐
I am committed to hard work – not easy fixes.	☐	☐
I practise something until I get better – rather than give up.	☐	☐
Career development is important to me.	☐	☐
I want to understand more fully why I do certain things.	☐	☐
I can improve how I make decisions.	☐	☐
I am committed to an ongoing process of self-development.	☐	☐
I see myself as much as a 'student' as a 'teacher'.	☐	☐
Totals		

Now total up your answers for each column.

Score interpretation

A score of more 'agrees' than 'disagrees' (>11) means that you are probably ready to be your own coach. However, you will need to work at it. Use the chapters of this book as a guide. Review areas where you need extra support, and get it.

A score of 15 or more 'agrees' shows a strong propensity for self-coaching and the process should come easily to you. But remember: this is a challenging and ongoing journey of self-development and awareness.

If you scored more 'disagrees' than 'agrees' (>11), then you probably are not yet ready to be your own leadership coach. With a little more reflection and effort, you could be there. Use the chapters of this book as a guide. Review areas where you need extra support, and get it.

A score of 15 or more 'disagrees' shows little support for you being your own coach. Have you completed this activity before working through the whole workbook? Consider going back and reviewing all the chapters before this one.

Now that you are in the final chapter of this workbook, take some time to evaluate where you are now. What skills do you believe you have as a leader? These skills may have developed over a long time or they may be new and even based on what you have learned about yourself in this workbook. Complete the checklist below to develop and strengthen your *existing* leadership skills.

COACHING SESSION 84

Develop and strengthen your existing leadership skills

Complete this checklist by indicating whether you presently have the leadership skill listed or whether you need to develop that skill. You can tick both boxes if this applies to you.

Leadership skill	I am competent at this skill	I need to develop this skill
Self-awareness	☐	☐
Time management	☐	☐
Delegation	☐	☐
Stress management	☐	☐
Verbal communication	☐	☐
Non-verbal communication	☐	☐
Written communication	☐	☐

Leadership skill	I am competent at this skill	I need to develop this skill
Active listening	☐	☐
Delegation	☐	☐
Team leadership	☐	☐
Motivating myself	☐	☐
Motivating others	☐	☐
Managing conflict	☐	☐
Cross-cultural leadership	☐	☐
Emotional Intelligence	☐	☐
Decision making	☐	☐
Avoiding groupthink	☐	☐
Performance management	☐	☐
People management	☐	☐
Self-management	☐	☐

CAREER PLANNING

In Chapter 6 we looked at SWOT analysis. This commonly used planning tool can also be used for personal career planning. You will remember that SWOT analysis looks at strengths and weaknesses in the internal environment and opportunities and threats in the external environment. If we apply this to career planning, it would look like Figure 13.1:

A completed template for a fictitious team leader may look like this:

Your internal strengths	Your internal weaknesses
Your external opportunities	Your external threats

Figure 13.1 Personal career SWOT

Internal career strengths	Internal career weaknesses
I have a good degree	Poor at time management
Good at delegation	14-month gap in job history
Excellent technical knowledge	Limited people-management experience
Can work under pressure	Not good at job interviews
Can speak two languages	No overseas experience
Good written communication	Presentation skills are poor
Good at working in a team	Easily bored
Strong at project management	
Completed the Leadership Coach workbook	
External career opportunities	**External career threats**
New position becoming available in department	The recession
About to finish MBA	People who have MBAs and overseas experience
My family contacts	Many competitors with more experience
Shortage of MBAs in my field	Two colleagues who are also completing MBA and will go for same new position
Course offered by my employer	
New mentoring programme	
I live in London	
My network	

COACHING SESSION 85

Personal career SWOT

Now complete the following template for yourself. Try to put something in every box. As a result of performing this analysis, you should be able to focus on your strengths, minimize your weaknesses, and take advantage of opportunities available to you.

SWOT template	
Strengths	Weaknesses
Opportunities	Threats
Conclusions	

COACHING OTHERS

The essence of the coaching process is two-way conversation. In this workbook, this has been between you and the coaching sessions. In your organization, it should be between you as a leader and your employees or colleagues. This should be a process that will lead to a commitment to improve performance or competency in a designated area. You can coach people in many areas, including:

- job performance
- time management
- strategy
- motivation
- change management
- emotional intelligence
- specific job skills

- communication skills
- delegation
- teamwork
- conflict management
- cross-cultural skills
- decision making
- other?

COACHING SESSION 86

Coaching others

Consider a person you know who would be willing to receive coaching. Why not pass on what you have learned in this workbook to another person? Make your notes in the form below.

Coaching plan	
Whom I will coach	
What I will coach them about? (Be specific – remember: SMART.)	
What does this person presently know about this?	

Coaching plan	
How open are they to coaching on this?	
Get commitment.	
Agree a time/location.	
Agree goals (Use SMART goals if possible.)	
Coach. (Remember to explain, demonstrate and review.)	
How did it go?	
Follow up and feedback on your coaching (make sure you get this from the coachee).	

CONCLUSION

In this workbook you have read a lot of new ideas and been introduced to many interesting concepts. By completing the coaching sessions and assessments, you should have learned many practical skills that will enhance your leadership abilities and give you the knowledge you need to update your 'leadership software'. With any luck, the book is now messy with lots of notes, comments, annotations and even disagreements.

If the book has done its job, you will have developed your skills as a leader. The author R.D. Cumming is quoted as saying: 'A good book has no ending', meaning that it should connect to the reader, increase their knowledge and inform them, but that it should also leave the reader feeling that they have more to learn. I hope this is what this workbook has achieved.

ACTION PLAN

Use this page to write out any final notes you have now that you have completed this workbook:

_____

_____

_____

_____

_____

_____

_____

_____

_____

_____

_____

_____

_____

_____

_____

_____

Developing your leadership skills is an ongoing journey. It is essential to your learning process to think about the skills you have developed by working through this workbook. Take some time to reflect on what you now know and what you still need to know. The next coaching session is the last one in this workbook and one of the most important. Complete it now.

COACHING SESSION 87

Audit your new leadership skills

What skills have you developed by working through this workbook? Complete the table below to assist you in assessing your new learning.

What I have learned from this workbook (Go back and look through the chapters now.)	1. 2. 3. 4. 5.
Areas I need to research or study more (Make a list – then act on it.)	1. 2. 3. 4. 5.

HELP DESK

Below is a summary of the learning outcomes in this book. Use it as an aide-memoire to make sure that you are covering all the bases.

Introduction to leadership

- Know the various theories and approaches to leadership study.
- Learn about transformational and transactional leadership theory.
- Understand the differences between leadership and management.

Time management and delegation

- Learn how to improve your time management.
- Acquire ways to improve your use of email.
- Understand the importance of maintaining a work–life balance.
- Understand the importance of delegation.

Communication skills

- Understand that many of the difficulties experienced in organizations are due to communication problems.
- Learn about non-verbal communication and some of the common myths about 'body language'.
- Learn how to improve your listening skills.

Barriers to communication

- Know that communication is not always perfect – problems can easily arise
- Understand that are many barriers to communication.

Teams and teamwork

- Understand how teams are formed.
- Know what makes a team effective.
- Learn how to build an effective team.
- Discover how team building helps a team develop competencies.

Strategy and strategic thinking

- Understand the difficulties faced when trying to define strategy.
- Learn how strategy can be applied to different levels of an organization.
- Realize the importance of having a clear strategy.
- Acquire the tools you can use to think about strategy.

Motivation

- Learn how to motivate the people you lead and how to motivate yourself.
- Understand the three key theories of motivation that have 'real-world' application.
- Realize how rewarding employees for achieving can be much more effective than punishing them for failing.
- Learn how to set and achieve SMART goals in you work and home life.

Managing workplace conflict

- Realize that conflict is an important and necessary part of life.
- Understand that conflict can be both constructive and destructive.
- Learn how to reframe your perception of conflict.

Leading change

- Understand the importance of managing change effectively.
- Consider the impact of change on organizations and individuals.
- Understand how approaches to change management need to take into account the individual.
- Learn how the 'Five Phases of Change' model can serve as a useful diagnostic tool to support and lead people

Cross-cultural leadership

- Think about the nature of culture and how to develop a definition of your own culture.
- Understand how we develop our personal cultural make-up.
- Learn about the six most prominent levels of culture.
- Discover how to improve cross-cultural communication.

Emotional intelligence (EI)

- Understand what emotional intelligence (EI) is and why it matters.
- Learn about the EI competence framework
- Know what the essential educational credentials are for a leader.
- Discover how to increase your own emotional intelligence (EI).

Leadership decision making

- Understand what leadership decision making is and why it is important.
- Learn how to use appropriate leadership decision-making techniques.
- Discover how to use practical tools such as brainstorming, the Crawford Slip Method and PMI.
- Know what groupthink is and how to recognize and avoid it when making decisions.

Becoming your own leadership coach

- Learn how to apply all you have learned in this workbook to becoming your own leadership coach.

SUGGESTED READING AND REFERENCES

Adams, J.S. (1963). Toward an understanding of inequity. *Journal of Abnormal and Social Psychology*, 67: 422–36.

Allan, K. and Burridge, K. (2006). *Forbidden Words: Taboo and the censoring of language*. Cambridge: Cambridge University Press.

Alderfer, C.P. (1969). An empirical test of a new theory of human needs. *Organisational Behavior and Human Performance*, 4: 142–75.

Adelson, M. (1970). Technology of forecasting. In C.S. Wallia (ed.), *Toward Century 21: Technology, society, and human values*. New York: Basic Books.

Ambrose M.L. and Kulik, C.T. (1999). Old friends, new faces: motivation research in the 1990s. *Journal of Management*, 25/3: 231–92.

Arnold, J., Cooper, C.L. and Robertson, I.Y. (1998). *Work Psychology: Understanding human behaviour in the workplace*. London: Financial Times Pitman Publishing.

Arnstein, C. (1982). Credentialism: why we have diploma mills. *Phi Della Kappan*, 68: 550–52.

Avruch, K. and Black, P. (1993). Conflict resolution in intercultural settings: problems and prospects. In D. Sandole and H. Van der Merwe (eds), *Conflict Resolution Theory and Practice: Integration and application*. New York: St. Martin's Press.

Bakalis, N. (2005). *Handbook of Greek Philosophy: From Thales to the Stoics – analysis and fragments*. Bloomington, IN: Trafford Publishing.

Barnes, J. (2007). *John F. Kennedy on Leadership: The lessons and legacy of a president*. New York: AMACOM.

Bass, B.M. (1985). *Leadership and Performance*. New York: Free Press.

Bass, B.M. (1998). *Transformational Leadership: Industrial, military and educational impact*. Mahway, NJ: Lawrence Erlbaum Associates.

Bass, B.M. (1990). *Bass and Stogdill's Handbook of Leadership*, 3rd edn. New York: Free Press.

Bass, B.M. and Avolio, B.J. (1994). *Improving Organizational Effectiveness through Transformational Leadership*. Thousand Oaks, CA: Sage Publications.

Baxter, C. (1999). *Field Marshal Bernard Law Montgomery, 1887–1976: A selected bibliography*. Westport, CT: Greenwood Press.

Belbin, R. (1981). *Management Teams: Why they succeed or fail*. London: Elsevier.

Belbin, R.M. (1993). *Team Roles at Work*. Oxford: Butterworth-Heinemann.

Bennis, W. (1998). *On Becoming a Leader*. London: Arrow.

Bennis, W. and Nanus, B. (1977). *Leaders: The strategies for taking charge.* New York: HarperCollins.

Boyatzis, R.E., Cowan, S.S. and Kolb, D.A. (1995*). Innovations in Professional Education: Steps on a journey to learning.* San Francisco: Jossey-Bass.

Burnes, B. (2000). *Managing Change: A strategic approach to organizational dynamics.* Upper Saddle River, NJ: Prentice Hall.

Buon, T. and Compton, R. (1990). Credentials, credentialism and employee selection. *Asia Pacific Human Resource Management*, 28: 126–32.

Buon, T. (1994). The recruitment of training professionals. *Training and Development in Australia* 21/5: 17–22.

Buon, T. (2007). *Employee Drug Use and EAPs. Employee Benefits.* UK.

Buon, T. (2008). Perspectives on managing workplace conflict. In A. Kinder, R. Hughes and C. Cooper (eds), *Employee Well-being Support: A workplace resource.* Hoboken, NJ: John Wiley and Sons.

Buon, T. and Compton, R.L. (1990). The development of alcohol and other drug programs in the workplace. *Journal Occupational Health and Safety – Australia and New Zealand*, 6/4: 264–77.

Burnes, B. (2004). *Managing Change: A strategic approach to organisational dynamics,* 4th edn. Upper Saddle River, NJ: Prentice Hall Publishing.

Burns, J.M. (1978). *Leadership.* New York: Harper & Raw.

Cardwell, M. (1996). *Dictionary of Psychology.* Chicago: Fitzroy Dearborn.

CIA World Factbook (2012).

Cole, G. (2002). *Personnel and Human Resource Management,* 5th edn. New York and London: Continuum.

Cook, R (1998). Managing international assignments. Unpublished monograph from Global Excellence www.global-excellence.com/

Covey, S., Merrill, A. and Merrill, R. (1994). *First Things First: To live, to love, to learn, to leave a legacy.* New York: Simon & Schuster.

Dalkey, N.C. and Helmer, O. (1963). An experimental application of the Delphi method to the use of experts. *Management Science* (April): 102.

de Bono, E. (1982). *De Bono's Thinking Course.* New York: Barnes & Noble.

Deci, E.L. (1971), Effects of externally mediated rewards on intrinsic motivation. *Journal of Personality and Social Psychology*, 18: 105–15.

Deci, E.L., and Ryan, R.M. (1985). *Intrinsic Motivation and Self-determination in Human Behavior.* New York: Plenum.

Deutsch, M. and Coleman, P.T (eds) (2000). *The Handbook of Conflict Resolution: Theory and practice.* Jossey-Bass Publishers: San Francisco.

Doran, G.T. (1981). There's a S.M.A.R.T. way to write management's goals and objectives. *Management Review*, 70/11: 35–6.

Davies, P. (1996). *About Time: Einstein's Unfinished Revolution.* New York: Simon & Schuster.

Ewing, D.W. (1977). *Freedom inside the Organization: Bringing civil Liberties to the workplace.* New York: Dutton.

Furnham, A., Steele, H., Pendleton, D. et al. (1993). A psychometric assessment of the Belbin team-role self-perception inventory. Author's reply. *Journal of Occupational and Organisational Psychology*, 66/3: 245–61.

Fortado, B. (2001). The metamorphosis of workplace conflict. *Human Relations*, 54: 9.

Gershon, D. (2006). The practice of empowerment. In T. Devane and P. Holman (eds), *The Change Handbook*, 2nd edn. San Francisco, CA: Berrett Koehler.

Ginott, H.G. (1969), *Between Parent and Teenager.* New York: Scribner.

Goleman, D. (1995). *Emotional Intelligence: Why it can matter more than IQ.* New York: Bantam.

Goleman, D. (1999). *Working with Emotional Intelligence.* London: Bloomsbury.

Gray, J. (2012). *Men Are from Mars, Women Are from Venus: A practical guide for improving communication and getting what you want in your relationships*, reissue edn. London: Harper Element.

Gray, J. and Starke, F. (1988). *Organizational Behaviour*, 4th edn (Columbus OH: Merrill.

Griffin, J., Boardman, J. and Murray, O. (2001). *The Oxford History of Greece and the Hellenistic World.* Oxfordshire: Oxford University Press.

Gribbin, J. (1996). *Companion to the Cosmos.* Universities Press (India) Pvt. Limited.

Guay, F., Chanal, J., Ratelle, C.F., Marsh, H.W., Larose, S., and Boivin, M. (2010). Intrinsic, identified, and controlled types of motivation for school subjects in young elementary school children. *British Journal of Educational Psychology*, 80/4: 711–35.

Guest, D. (1984). What's new in motivation, *Personnel Management* (May).

Gupta, A. (2009). TED Talks: India's hidden hotbeds of invention. Filmed Nov 2009, posted May 2010, TEDIndia. www.ted.com/talks/anil_gupta_india_s_hidden_hotbeds_of_invention.html

Herring, S. (1994). Gender differences in computer-mediated communication: Bringing familiar baggage to the new frontier, Miami: American Library Association annual convention – keynote talk, 27 June 1994.

Herzberg, F. (1959), *The Motivation to Work*. New York: John Wiley and Sons.

Herzberg, F. (1982). *The Managerial Choice*: *To be efficient and to be human*. Salt Lake City, UT: Olympus Publishing.

Herzberg, F. (1987). One more time: How do you motivate employees? *Harvard Business Review*, 65/5 (Sept/Oct).

Hofstede, G.J. (1980). *Culture's Consequences*. Beverly Hills, CA: Sage.

Hofstede, G. (1984). *Culture's Consequences: International differences in work-related values*, abridged edn. London: Sage.

Hofstede, G. (1991). *Cultures and Organizations*. New York: McGraw-Hill.

Isaacson, J. (2011). *Steve Jobs*. New York: Simon & Schuster.

ILO/WHO. (1987). *Responses to drug and Alcohol Problems in the Workplace*. Geneva: World Health Organization.

Irving, J. (1972). *Victims of Groupthink*. Boston, MA: Houghton Mifflin.

Irving, J. (1982). *Groupthink*, 2nd edn. Boston, MA: Houghton Mifflin.

Johson, G. and Scholes, K. (1989). *Exploring Corporate Strategy*. Cambridge: Cambridge University Press.

Kanter, R.M. (1984). *The Change Masters: Innovation and entrepreneurship in the American corporation*. New York: Simon & Schuster.

Kaplan, R.S. and Norton, D.P. (1992). The balanced scorecard: measures that drive performance. *Harvard Business Review* (Jan/Feb): 71–80.

Kelly, M. (2011). To talk or not talk – the walk to the meeting room. 7 April 2011. http://www.kellyspeech.com.au/2011/04

Kluger, K. (2013). The art of living. *Time*, Europe edn (23 Sept).

Kotter, J.P. (1990). *A Force for Change: How leadership differs from management*. New York: Free Press.

Kübler-Ross, E. (1969), *On Death and Dying*. London: Routledge.

Lewin, K., Lippitt, R. and White, R.K. (1939). Patterns of aggressive behaviour in experimentally created social climates. *Journal of Social Psychology*, 10: 271–99.

Lao, Tzu (1992). *Lao Tzu: Te-Tao Ching: a new translation based on the recently discovered Ma-wang-tui texts*, Classics of Ancient China, trans. R.G. Henricks. New York: Ballantine Books.

Locke, E.A. and Bryan, J. (1968). Goal setting as a determinant of the effects of knowledge of score in performance. *American Journal of Psychology*, 81: 398–406.

Locke, E.A. (1996). Motivation through conscious goal setting. *Applied and Preventive Psychology*, 5: 117–24.

Locke, E.A. (1997). The motivation to work: what we know. In M. Maehr and P. Pintrich (eds), *Advances in Motivation and Achievement*, vol. 10, pp. 375–412. Greenwich, CT: JAI Press.

Locke, E.A. and Latham, P.G. (1990). *A Theory of Goal Setting and Task Performance*. Englewood Cliffs, NJ: Prentice-Hall.

Machiavelli, Niccolò (1961). *The Prince*, trans. George Bull. London: Penguin. Markides, C. (1999). A dynamic view of strategy. *Sloan Management Review*, 40 (Spring): 55–63.

Makagonova, V. (2013). Top 10 myths about Russia – Russian myths. Russia Travel/About.com http://gorussia.about.com/od/Russian_history_and_culture/tp/Top-10-Russian- Myths.htm

Maslow, A.H. (1943). A theory of human motivation. *Psychological Review*, 50: 370–96.

Maslow, A.H. (1954). *Motivation and Personality*. New York: Harper & Row.

McClelland, D. (1961). *The Achieving Society*. NJ: Van Nostrand.

McGregor, D. (1961). *The Human Side of Enterprise*. New York: McGraw-Hill.

Mayer, J.D., Salovey, P., Caruso, D.R. and Sitarenios, G. (2003). Measuring emotional intelligence with the MSCEIT V2.0. *Emotion*: 3, 97–105.

Mehrabian, A. and Ferris, S.R. (1967), Inference of attitudes from nonverbal communication in two channels. *Journal of Consulting Psychology*, 31/3: 48–258.

Mehrabian, A. and Wiener, M. (1967). Decoding of inconsistent communications, *Journal of Personality and Social Psychology*, 6: 109–14.

Mehrabian, A. (2009). www.kaaj.com/psych/smorder.html

Moorhead, G. and Griffin, R.W. (1998). *Organizational Behavior: Managing people and organizations*, 5th edn. Boston, MA: Houghton Mifflin.

Nakane, I. (2007). *Silence in Intercultural Communication: Perceptions and performance*, Pragmatics and Beyond New Series. John Benjamins Publishing.

NHS (2013). Communication problems and support – Care and support (available at www.nhs.uk/CarersDirect/guide/communication/Pages/Communicating.aspx)

Osborn, A.F. (1942). *How to Think Up*. New York: McGraw Hill.

Osborn, A.F. (1963). *Applied Imagination: Principles and procedures of creative problem-solving*. New York: Scribner.

Payne, W.L. (1985). A study of emotion: developing emotional intelligence; self- integration; relating to fear, pain and desire (theory, structure of reality, problem- solving, contraction/expansion, tuning in/comingout/letting go). Doctoral dissertation, Cincinnati, OH: The Union for Experimenting Colleges and Universities.

Porter, M.E. (1980). *Competitive Strategy: Techniques for analyzing industries and competitors.* New York: The Free Press.

Sargent, J.F. (1992). 5 gender stereotypes that used to be the exact opposite. http://www.cracked.com/article_19780

Saunders, D. (1992). 10 myths about Muslims in the West. On-line blog. http://www.huffingtonpost.com/doug-saunders/10-myths-about-muslims-in_b_1864589.html

Stogdill, R.M. (1948). Personal factors associated with leadership: A survey of the literature, *Journal of Psychology*, 25: 35–71.

Swailes, S. and McIntyre-Bhatty, T. (2002). The 'Belbin' team role inventory: reinterpreting reliability estimates, *Journal of Managerial Psychology*, 17.6: 529–36.

Tang, S.-H. and Hall, V.C. (1995). The overjustification effect: a meta-analysis. *Applied Cognitive Psychology*, 9: 365–404.

The Economist, 20 March 1993: 106.

The Original Australian Test of Intelligence www.wilderdom.com/personality

Tannenbaum, R. and Schmidt, W.H. 1973 [reprint edn 2009]. *How to Choose a Leadership Pattern*, Harvard Business Review Classics (Cambridge, MA: Harvard Business School).

Thorndike, R.L. and Stein, S. (1937). An evaluation of the attempts to measure social intelligence. *Psychological Bulletin*, 34: 275–84.

Tidwell, A.C. (1998). *Conflict Resolved?* London: Pinter.

Tuckman, B.W. (1965). Developmental sequence in small groups *Psychological Bulletin*, 63/6: 384–99.

Tuckman, B.W. and Jensen, M.A.C. (1977). Stages of small-group development revisited, *Group and Organization Management*, 2/4: 419–27.

Vroom, V.H. (1964). *Work and Motivation.* New York: Wiley.

Vroom, V.H. and Yetton, P.W. (1973). *Leadership and Decision-making.* Pittsburgh: University of Pittsburgh Press.

Vroom, V.H. and Jago, A.G. (1988). *The New Leadership: Managing participation in organizations.* Englewood Cliffs, NJ: Prentice Hall.

Wahba, M.A. and Bridwell, L.G. (1976). Maslow reconsidered: a review of research on the need hierarchy theory. *Organisational Behaviour and Human Performance*, 15: 212–40.

Watts, A.G. (1985). Education and employment: The traditional bonds. In R. Dale (ed.), *Education Training and Employment: Toward a new vocationalism.* Oxford: Pergamon Press, pp. 9–22.

Weeks, D. (1994). *The Eight Essential Steps to Conflict Resolution*. New York: Tarcher/ Putman.

Wiersma, U.J. (1992). The effects of extrinsic rewards in intrinsic motivation: A meta-analysis. *Journal of Occupational and Organisational Psychology*, 65: 101–14.

Wood, J. (2009). *Gendered Lives: Communication, gender, and culture*, 8th edn. Belmont, CA: Wadsworth Publishing.

Yammarino F.J., Dionne, S.D., Chun. J.U. and F. Dansereau (2005). Leadership and levels of analysis: a state-of-the-science review. *Leadership Quarterly*, 16: 879–919.

Zaleznik, A. (1997). Managers and leaders: are they different? *Harvard Business Review*, 55: 67–78.

INDEX